ON YA
WARNIE

TOTALLY UNAUTHORISED & UNCENSORED

KEN PIESSE

Published by:
Wilkinson Publishing Pty Ltd
ACN 006 042 173
Level 4, 2 Collins Street, Melbourne, Vic 3000
Ph: 03 9654 5446
www.wilkinsonpublishing.com.au

National Library of Australia Cataloguing-in-Publication data:

Piesse, Ken.
       On Ya Warnie : The laughs, legends, loves, bets, beans, matches, mates, phones, parties, stats, stuff-ups, umpires.

       ISBN 9781921332173 (pbk.).

       1. Warne, Shane. 2. Cricket players - Australia -
       Biography. 3. Cricket - Australia. 4. Cricket - Bowling -
       Biography. I. Title.

       796.358092

Illustrator and cover design: Paul Harvey
Design: Michael Bannenberg
Printed in Australia by Trojan Press

Contents

Sabina Park, 1995: Brian Lara, c Healy, b. Warne 65, fourth Test

Preface

One of our great sportswriters Garry Linnell once called Don Bradman Mary McKillop with pads on. He was the patron saint of cricket, a squeaky-clean hero whose following has endured.

Shane Warne is equally-loved for his contribution to the game. He reminded us all just how lethal spin bowling can be.

The Don was the ultimate Invincible and Warnie is the ultimate Annihilator, his match-winning presence demoralising the opposition.

The Sheik of Tweak steamrolled opponents and electrified the game, attracting new streams of popularity.

Men admire him for his sportsmanship and grit and women are attracted by his good looks and movie star status.

His life on and off the field has been an exhilarating rollercoaster of controversy and acclaim. He is a world famous celebrity who has socialised with the rich and famous, from Lady Di, the Queen, rock stars, super models and the who's who in business and sport. The glamour and hype has been extraordinary and at times he's lived outside the square, dazzled by the bright lights and the red carpet.

He's unable to do normal, everyday activities without causing a stir, or being chased by the Paparazzi. Every joke or harmless aside is heard around the world, every mistake exaggerated and magnified.

He exudes charisma and has an endearing, open manner towards his fans.

His charity work, much of it under the umbrella of the Shane Warne Foundation sees him looking after the sick and disadvantaged. He dotes after his three kids and is a good family man.

In the public domain, whatever the controversy, he's still Warnie. Whatever his escapades, people still are drawn to him, celebrate with him, and yes, thousands admire him.

He's the ultimate champion of his generation and Australia's most significant sportsman since the Don. We love him. On ya Warnie.

Introduction

$\mathscr{E}$dgbaston, 2005. The rowdies in the Eric Hollies Stand are in full voice, chanting and singing and bathing in England's long-awaited Ashes dominance. Barmy Army songbooks are in abundance as the choruses are belted out with the gusto of Freddie Flintoff's six-hitting.

From the apparently-harmless ditties directed at anyone wearing green and gold like *You All Live in a Convict Colony* (sung to *Yellow Submarine*), the mob gets nasty and targets Australia's supremo Shane Warne with "Where's You're Missus Gone? Far, Far, Away" (to *Chirpy Chirpy Cheep Cheep*).

It's meant to be fun, but the delivery is venomous and increasingly uncouth and the Australians bristle for their mate, whose marriage to the love-of-his-life Simone had lurched to a new low, according to the London tabloids.

Rather than being demoralized by the rowdies, Warne is in his own unsinkable zone, and runs through England's middle order with the finest bowling of his headlining career. After every wicket – and he is to claim six this unforgettable Saturday in Birmingham – he grins, doffs his hat and slowly and very ceremoniously bows in the direction of the mob, inciting fresh howls of abuse.

Australia is to lose the Test in one of the greatest finishes but in the end, there's not even a boundary in it.

Once again, even under the most intense personal fire, Warne had shown himself to be cricket's most magnetic personality, a showman supreme and a competitor as feisty as any to wear the baggy green.

Much of his personal life may have been a botch and while

not everyone may have agreed with his *joie de vivre*, the changing hair-dos or the body jewellery, we all celebrated during those momentous Test weeks in England his charisma, performance and sheer ability.

Without Warne in '05, there was no possible way Australia could still have clung onto the Ashes, even into the final afternoon of a summer which turned pear-shaped at Edgbaston when Glenn McGrath trod on a ball during a casual warm-up with reserve 'keeper Brad Haddin.

Our Australian support group had only just been admitted after high-security queueing and we were walking around the ground past the secondhand bookstall to our vantage spots when an ashen-faced McGrath was wheeled directly past us to an ambulance, his Test over even before it had started.

Without his champion side-kick, Warne had stood taller than ever before, shouldering fresh responsibility with bat and ball and all but snatching a remarkable win in the greatest modern-times Test of all.

It made you proud to be from the same city.

From a party boy who just happened to spin the ball like a top and was fast tracked into teams he initially had no right to be in, Warne's genius revived an ailing art and ensured fresh fanfare for the greatest game of all.

Kids of all ages started to pack a cricket ball into their lunch boxes and spin it at every opportunity. They doused their noses in sun cream, mimicked Warnie's short-stepped run-up and attempted to bowl flippers and zootas just like their hero.

Like tens of thousands of Australians, I'd watched the Warne phenomenon grow like no other.

I'd seen it all from first hand; we'd lived in adjourning suburbs and shared many of the same cricketing friends.

As a slightly chubby 16-year-old he'd ripped a leg-break past me and seen me stumped by yards in a match at Mentone Grammar. I'd been at the other end taking his leg breaks in my bare hands as a *Sunday Press* photographer snapped away merrily at Melbourne's inner-city Albert Ground. The ball was still new and the stitches ripped into my hands, leaving indents.

I'd written two books about him and he'd contributed forewords to two of mine, including *Down at the Junction*, St Kilda's

150 year history, a ground where he'd first told the practice coach he was a batsman who also liked to bowl a few leggies.

Later that morning the club's captain Shaun Graf asked what the showy kid with the peroxided hair had said he did.

"Not sure about his batting," he said, "but he can bowl a bit."

It was the beginning of a phenomenon, a scene-stealing career which saw Warne and cricket dominate the front pages like never before, even in the Bradman years.

Warne was the magician, the joker in the pack, the go-to

man, the high-spirited super power of Australian cricket and from conducting corroboree dances on dressing room balconies to zipping his sports cars down the MCG's Brunton Avenue. He did everything flat-out.

With Warne in their team, Australia was virtually unbeatable. No-one, not even Don Bradman, won more cricket matches for Australia.

Australian sport's ultimate headliner, he changed cricket like never before.

This summer, for the first in 15, he may be onlooking, but he's still making headlining statements in the papers, is upfront on the TV and via the new VB talking doll, on mantels and bedside tables right around the country.

On Ya Warnie celebrates Australia's finest and most charismatic sportsman since Keith Miller and features the yarns, the laughs, the flippers, the fancies – and much, much more.

Hope it brings a smile to your dial.

My thanks, in particular, to Jon Anderson and Mark Browning, Robert Craddock, statisticians Charles Davis and Ross Dundas, photographer Patrick Eagar, cartoonist Paul Harvey and Jon Pierik. for their contributions.

KEN PIESSE, Melbourne

*"He's probably
the greatest cricketer
who has ever been."*
RICKY PONTING

Warnie: A Sneak Peek

FULL NAME: Shane Keith Warne

BIRTHDATE: 13 September, 1969

BIRTHPLACE: Ferntree Gully (Melbourne)

HEIGHT: 183cm

FAMILY: Father Keith, Mother Brigitte, Brother Jason, Daughters Brooke and Summer, Son Jackson

MARRIED: (to Simone) 1995

DIVORCED: 2006

OCCUPATION: Cricketer

LIVES AT: Brighton (Victoria, Australia) and Southhampton (UK)

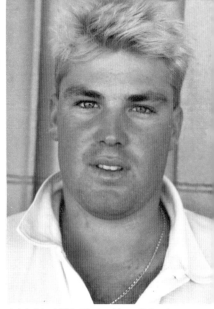

Adelaide, 1991. Photo: Moss Seigert

CRICKET SKILLS: Right-arm leg-spin, flippers, zootas, googlies, toppies, back-spinners and one or two variations of the theme; right-hand No.8 batsman

NICKNAMES: Twistie, Showbags, Young Barks, Hollywood, Truman, Elvis, The Sheik of Tweak, Suicide, The Sultan of Spin, Warnie

HEROES: Dennis Lillee, Rod Marsh, Ian Botham, Ian Chappell (cricket), Dermott Brereton, Trevor Barker (football)

FIRST JOB: Delivering beds for *Forty Winks*

CLUBS/TEAMS: Brighton, St Kilda, Knowle, Imperials, Glenelg, Victoria, Hampshire, ICC World XI, Australia

MAJOR MENTORS: Shaun Graf, Allan Border, Ian Chappell, Terry Jenner (his long-time coach), Bob Simpson (showed him the value of going around the wicket)

INJURIES: Broken legs, finger, thumb, shoulder, knee

OTHER SPORTS ENJOYED: Football (follows St Kilda FC), golf

FAVORITE GROUNDS: MCG, SCG, The 'Gabba, Lord's, Old Trafford

LEAST FAVORED GROUND: The WACA

FAVORITE FOOD: Baked beans, tinned spaghetti, toasted cheese sandwiches, jelly snakes, thick shakes

FIRST WICKET: Ravi Shastri ((India), Sydney, 1992

LAST WICKET: Andrew Flintoff (England), Sydney, 2007

BEST WICKET: Mike Gatting (England), Old Trafford, 1993

BEST SHOT PLAYED: The inside out slash over point.

BEST SHOT PLAYED AGAINST: Chris Cairns (New Zealand), Hamilton (a well-pitched leg spinner which disappeared for six a long way back, over square leg)

BOOKS AUTHORED:

Shane Warne My Own Story as told to Mark Ray (Swan Publishing, 1997), *Shane Warne My Autobiography* with Richard Hobson (Hodder & Stoughton, 2001), *Shane Warne My Complete Illustrated Career, The Official Edition* with Richard Hobson (Cassell Illustrated, 2007)

LIFE AFTER CRICKET: Commentary, coaching, appearances, investment, philanthropy (Shane Warne Foundation), mates, the good life, being Dad.

Warnie, A to Z

From Arjuna to Zimbabwe, a Warnie alphabet

A: Is for Arjuna Ranatunga, the portly Sri Lankan captain who irritated Warnie like no other. And he continued to get under his skin, too, in retirement.

B: Is for Baked Beans, one of Warnie's staple foods especially whenever his passport pointed towards India, Pakistan and Sri Lanka. Box after box would be flown in, courtesy of the boys from SPC in Melbourne. **B** is also for Brereton, Dermott Brereton and Barker, Trevor Barker, two of his boyhood heroes.

C: Is for Cullinan – Daryll Cullinan – the richly-talented South African batsman with a Warne phobia, so serious that he once visited a sports psychologist to see if his problem was all mental. He averaged 48 against all other comers but only 12 against the Aussies, prompting Warne to proclaim how he'd "love to bowl to Cullinan for a living". Warnie would invariably greet Cullinan with: "C'mon Daryll let's see out if we can get you back on that leather couch again".

> *'Go and deflate yourself, you balloon'*

Cullinan occasionally hit back: "Go and deflate yourself, you balloon" was one retort. "Looks like you've been eating all those pies again," was another.

D: Is for Dick as in Dick Pound the anti-drugs crusader. He wanted Warnie banned for two years and couldn't understand why he wasn't after Warne was found guilty of taking banned drugs during the summer of 2002-03. Pound didn't care two hoots that they were only slimming pills.

E: Is for the "Earl of Twirl", Warnie's spin partner of the '90s, Tim May. **E** is also for earring. Warnie was one of the first leading high-profile sportsmen, along with basketball's Michael Jordan, to first wear one, a Nike swooch from one of his early sponsors.

F: Is for "Freddie" Flintoff, who just happened to be Warnie's last Test wicket, courtesy of an Adam Gilchrist stumping, Sydney, 2007.

G: Is for "Gatt", Mike Gatting, who was on strike for *that ball*, Warnie's "Ball of the Century" which swerved in before spinning wickedly to clip the top of his off stump at Old Trafford in 1993. It was his first ball in an Ashes Test. "It was just meant to be a warm-up ball, too," said Warnie.

H: Is for Hum. Face Warnie and you hear the ball coming at you. **H** is also for "Hollywood", Allan Border's nickname for Warnie.

I: Is for India, the only opponent Warne was unable to dominate during his spectacular career. In 14 Tests against them, he took just 43 wickets at an average close to 50.

J: Is for "John", the mysterious Indian bookmaker who successfully offered bribes to Warne and Mark Waugh for pitch conditions and weather reports in the mid-'90s. **J** is also for Jerry, Jerry Hall, one of his favourite, err... blonde models.

K: Is for Kolkata (formerly Calcutta) where he received the biggest mauling of his career, courtesy of cricketing fall-guy Mohammad Azharuddin and Co: none for 147 in six spells and 42 overs.

L: Is for Warnie's Lucky Pants; he'd pull them out of his kit if he was ever going through a lean trot. They weren't needed very often. **L** is also for Lord's, the spiritual home of cricket in St John's Wood, London, where Warne's portrait hangs in the Long Room bar. A portrait of fellow *Wisden* Cricketer of the Century Sir Donald Bradman is in the Lord's museum opposite the Ashes urn.

M: Is for Mobile phone, a piece of modern technology Warnie can't leave home without.

N: Is for Ninety-nine, Warne's highest Test score before he self-destructed to what should have been called no ball after New Zealand's Daniel Vettori over-stepped the front crease in Perth. "I'm sure Shane would have swapped 100 wickets for that one extra run," said Steve Waugh later.

O: Is for Openers; Warnie dismissed 104 of them, representing 15 per cent of his wickets.

P: Is for Pills, or more precisely the two banned diuretics Warne took to accelerate weight loss, resulting in a 12-month ban when he was at the height of his powers.

Q: Is for Pakistani charismatic leg-spinning maestro Abdul Qadir whose magical assortment of leggies, toppies and wrong-'uns helped inspire Warne to take up the trade.

R: Is for Richie Richardson who was famously flippered by Warne in Melbourne in '92. The look on the West Indian champ's face when he heard the "death rattle" remains an unforgettable memory of the day Warnie won his first Test downunder. **R** is also for Red 23, his favorite roulette number.

S: Is for the Sheik of Tweak (yet another Warnie nickname) and for Simone Callahan, the pretty blonde promotions girl from Ascot Vale he took a fancy to and eventually married. They'd first met in March 1992, at Royal Melbourne Golf Club during a Victorian cricket celebrity golf day. **S** is also for St Kilda the Melbourne Premier League club he represented so proudly for 20 years.

T: Is for Tamblyn, Mike Tamblyn, Warnie's old captain with Brighton seconds who told the 17-year-old to stick to his batting. Of his bowling, he said: "You haven't got it son."

U: Is for the Southampton Solent University which in 2006 awarded an honorary doctorate to Warne for his services to cricket. An honorary doctorate? Warnie? Amazing ... but true!

V: Is for Vanity. Warnie admitting he'd accepted pills from his mum so he could look slimmer in the face for the TV cameras. **V** is also for Vegemite, another Warnie staple.

W: Is for Woolloongabba, Brisbane's boutique Test venue – better known as The 'Gabba – and Warnie's most successful ground. He took 68 wickets at 20 there.

X: Is for the BMW X5 he now drives around Melbourne after once having a Ferrari, two BMW four-wheel drives, two Mercedes and a Holden VK Commodore at his opulent south of the Yarra home. In England he drives a Mercedes.

Y: Is for Year, as in the calendar year of 2005 when Warne took a record 96 wickets at 22.05 in just 15 Tests.

Z: Is for the single Test Warne played in Zimbabwe in 1999-2000. It was the 11th country he'd played Test cricket in … by comparison, Don Bradman played in just two.

LIFELONG MATES: Warnie with his St Kilda teammates Nick Jewell (standing), Graeme Rummans, Glenn Lalor and Michael Klinger during a Victorian second XI game, in 2004

Always The Showman

With his charisma and natural confidence, Warnie was a head turner from his early teens

*L*ike his boyhood hero, footballer Dermott Brereton, Warnie was a showman supreme and with his outgoing manner, boyish high spirits and endearing naivety, a perennial headliner.

From his teen years in school he liked to get on with everyone. He was always different, whether it was via his mullet hair-dos or insistence on wearing his cricket cap backwards, long before Lleyton Hewitt first said "C'mon!"

Once he arrived at school with a brand new Duncan Fearnley *Magnum*, but instead of a traditional navy blue or red grip, his was bright orange and yellow!

He wasn't a meat eater and amazed his school chums whenever they visited McDonald's by regularly discarding the hamburger and filling the bread roll with chips and a liberal dousing of tomato sauce.

> *'...the teeth whitening and the sun-bed tan were all to come.'*

A little like Elvis and his penchant for peanut butter and jelly sandwiches, Warnie's basic staple was buttered rolls with chips, toast and vegemite, baked beans and toasted cheese sandwiches. Hawaiian pizzas were a variation, but never with the pineapple.

Occasionally he'll also have spaghetti bolognaise, but without

Left: 1995, Queen's Park, Port of Spain, third one-day international. Photo: Ray Titus.

any trimmings whatsoever. Seafood was definitely a no-no.
Chicken, too.

One of his mates at Mentone Grammar, Raj Krishnan said he
couldn't remember Warnie once eating any vegetables.

"He liked the fast foods, complete with strawberry milkshakes.
He came around to our place a few times and my Mum asked if he
ever ate *decent* food!"

Another schoolmate Dean Jameson said Warne was
flamboyant, outspoken and easily distracted. They called him
"Twistie", after his strawberry blond hair or "Hollywood".

The fashionable clothes, blond streaks, jewellery, the teeth
whitening and the sun-bed tan were all to come. With his
matchwinning ways and Boys' Own charisma, he proved to be a
media dream.

Sydney, 1996: World Series winners

Shane by Shane I

QUESTION: "Shane, what do you think
of New Zealanders?"
SHANE WARNE: "They are all just frustrated Aussies".

"Take that @#$&ing shot back to Wales."
S.W. after dismissing England new boy Matthew Maynard at The Oval in 1993.

"I couldn't believe what I had heard
and said: 'You are @#$&ing kidding'."
S.W. to Salim Malik after being offered a bribe to bowl badly in Karachi.

"@#$&-off. Go on Hudson. @#$&-off out of here."
S.W. to South African opener Andrew Hudson, 1993-94.

"I hope he gets a duck in every innings he plays."
S.W on the bookmaker's pal, Pakistani's Salim Malik.

"I'm not arrogant. I have confidence in my ability.
Yes I'm emotional about my cricket. I'm competitive and
aggressive. I have to be. I'm a bowler and I'm in the
team to dismiss batsmen. That's what I'm paid to do."

"Some people just don't like the way you play.
I just go out and be myself. If people like me, great.
If not I'm not going to lose any sleep."

You Have Been Warned

The 25 greatest Test performances from the sultan of spin

1. AUGUST, 1992: 1st TEST v SRI LANKA, Colombo

It remains Australia's greatest ever "come from behind" win on tour. The Sri Lankans were just 36 runs short of a historic, first ever win against Australia at the Sinhalese Sports Club when captain Allan Border reintroduced his touring new chum, more in hope than faith. "Warm up Warnie. You're on next over," he called.

After his first innings' mauling, the kid's cumulative figures had blown to 1-335 in his first three Tests. Frontliner Asanka Gurusinha was set and the excitable Sri Lankan crowd starting to party. It seemed inconceivable that Sri Lanka wouldn't win.

> *... You've got the others, but I'm damned if you're going to get me!'*

However, Gurusinha lost the strike and in 13 balls, Warne grabbed three for none, including the last man, left-hander Ranjith Madurasinghe, with biting leg breaks which spun prodigiously from the footmarks of the bowlers at the opposite end.

In a miraculous comeback, the Aussies had snatched one of the great wins by just 16 runs. More boxes of beer had to be sent for from the Australian embassy. A star had been born.

"Hollywood (Warne) could have crawled into a corner and died, but he won us a Test match." said fellow spinner Greg

"Mo" Matthews. "And he didn't win it darting them in. He won it giving them a rip and tossing them up. He put his hand up when it mattered the most."

SCOREBOARD: *Australia 256 and 471 defeated Sri Lanka 8-547 dec. (A. Ranatunga 127, A.P. Gurusinha 137, R.S. Kaluwitharana 132, S.K. Warne 22-2-107-0) and 164 (S.K. Warne 5.1-3-11-3) by 16 runs. Warne Test No.3*

2. DECEMBER, 1992: 2nd TEST v WEST INDIES, Melbourne

Australia had not defeated the West Indies in a "live" rubber Test for 11 years. Chasing 359 on the last day on a placid pitch the Windies were in control at 1-143. In his first Test on his home ground, Warne had taken one wicket in the first innings and none in the second and was seriously wondering his right to be in the XI. After-all, he'd taken five wickets in five Tests at almost 100 runs apiece.

Walking down the hill from the Hilton that morning, Warne had been unusually silent and when asked by Ian Healy what was he thinking about, said: "I'm worried about being thumped all around the ground in front of my friends and never playing for Australia again."

Healy reassured him of his status in the team, told him to relax and simply enjoy himself.

West Indian captain Richie Richardson had reached his half century and was playing with growing certainty. Bowling his ninth over from the members end, Warne produced his deadly flipper, the faster one which skids and it zeroed straight through Richardson's defences before skidding into his off stump. At the time Richardson was the most acclaimed batsman in the world. He'd just been bowled by a tyro whose only thoughts a few hours previously had been just how big an embarrassment he was going to make of himself in front of his mates.

The rest of the Windies capitulated to Warne, the team losing 9-72 to go down by 139. Warne took seven of the nine wickets in 14 overs and was named Man of the Match.

Among his 700-plus wickets, the Richardson dismissal remains one of his all-time favorites.

SCOREBOARD: *Australia 395 (M.E. Waugh 112, A.R. Border 110) and 196 defeated West Indies 233 (S.K. Warne 24-7-65-1) and 219 (P.V. Simmons 110 S.K. Warne 23.2-8-52-7) by 139 runs. Warne Test No.5*

3. JUNE, 1993: 1st TEST v ENGLAND, Manchester

Warne's extraordinary first ball in Ashes cricket at Old Trafford is part of cricketing folklore. It drifted almost a metre and spun back drunkenly to glance the top of Mike Gatting's off stump. Gatting was stupefied and lingered in his forward defensive pose hardly believing he'd heard the death rattle. "He just stared down the pitch, then back at his stumps, in amazement," said umpire Dickie Bird who was at the bowler's end. Finally essaying a glance at the square leg umpire who confirmed he was indeed out, bowled, Gatting slowly trudged away, the victim of "The Ball of the Century".

That one ball set up Australia's summer and the Ashes were retained 4-1. Warne took 34 wickets in a succession of outstanding solos to be Australia's player of the series. "I was pumped up and rock'n'rolling," he said. "That one ball set the stage for all the things that ran for me throughout the series."

Gatting was the first of Warne's eight wickets for the match.

That night the players shared a drink and Gatting approached Warne. "Bloody hell, Warnie. What happened?"

"Sorry mate," he said, "I just got lucky."

He was Man of the Match.

SCOREBOARD: *Australia 289 (M.A. Taylor 124, P.M. Such 6-67) and 5-432 dec. (I.A. Healy 102 not out) defeated England 205 (S.K. Warne 24-10-51-4) and 332 (G.A. Gooch 133, S.K. Warne 49-26-86-4) by 179 runs. Warne Test No.12*

4. AUGUST, 1993: 5th TEST v ENGLAND, Birmingham

It's a tight Test on a turning Edgbaston pitch. The decisive moment arrives on the fourth day. Key English batsman Graham Gooch is on 48 and in control.

Operating around the wicket, Warnie turns a massive leg-break out of the rough and bowls Gooch behind his legs after the Englishman had attempted to kick the ball away.

Warne had talked the night before of bowling fuller to Gooch and hoping one could spin back far enough. "Gooch barely bothered with it," said Warne later. "He threw no more than a token pad at the ball. But I'd put plenty of spin on it and it pitched, bit back and took the leg stump. To see his wicket shatter was fantastic and I just lost control and ran at 'A.B.' (captain Allan Border) pointing at him and celebrating what I had just done."

It was a key, ever-so satisfying moment for Warne who from his earliest days as a fast-tracked spinner always said he wanted to take the important wicket that changed the fortunes of a match.

SCOREBOARD: *Australia 408 (M.E. Waugh 137) and 2-120 defeated England 276 (P.R. Reiffel 6-71 S.K. Warne 21-7-63-1) and 251 (T.B.A. May 5-89, S.K. Warne 49-23-82-5) by eight wickets. Warne Test No.16*

5. NOVEMBER, 1994: 1st TEST v ENGLAND, Brisbane

After Australian captain Mark Taylor declined to enforce the follow-on, England began the last day on 2-211 with major hopes of forcing a draw, even if 508 for the win seemed far-fetched. Within two overs, Warne changed the game when Alec Stewart was bowled by a flipper he thought was a long hop and Mike Atherton lbw to a full-length leg-break.

The English were marooned, hardly daring to venture outside their creases as Warne dismissed five of England's top six. Included, again, was Graham Gooch, England's lynchpin.

Congratulating him on his second innings 50, Warne said: "Well played Mr Gooch!"

"Thanks. You've got the others, but I'm damned if you're going to get me!"

Within 10 minutes Gooch had top-edged an attempted sweep, a key dismissal as England loss by 184 runs. Warne all but took a hat trick at the end before finishing with Test-best figures of 8-71. Again he was named Man of the Match.

SCOREBOARD: *Australia 426 (M.J. Slater 176, M.E. Waugh 140) and 8-248 dec. defeated England 167 (C.J. McDermott 6-53 S.K. Warne 21.2-7-39-3) and 323 (S.K. Warne 50.2-22-71-8) by 184 runs. Warne Test No.30*

6. DECEMBER, 1994: 2nd TEST v ENGLAND, Melbourne

Australia's crushing win in the Boxing Day Ashes Test was sealed by a Warne hat-trick, his first ever at any level, even going back to his days in the juniors at East Sandringham. It was also the first in an Anglo-Australian Test match for 91 years.

When umpire Steve Randell raised his finger to acknowledge

England No.11 Devon Malcolm's dismissal, courtesy of birthday boy David Boon's finger-tipper at short leg, the small crowd almost lifted the roof off the Great Southern Stand as they hailed the home town boy.

In the opening two Tests of the 1994-95 series, Warne had claimed an astonishing 20-190.

He winked at a mate afterwards in the rooms. "Think I'll wake up soon," he said.

SCOREBOARD: *Australia 279 and 7-320 dec. (D.C. Boon 131) defeated England 212 (S.K. Warne 27.4-8-64-6) and 92 (C.J. McDermott 5-42 S.K. Warne 13-6-16-3) by 295 runs. Warne Test No.31*

7. NOVEMBER, 1995: 1st TEST v PAKISTAN, Brisbane

"I felt justice had been done," Warne said of the dismissal of Salim Malik for a duck in Pakistan's second innings. Twelve months earlier, Malik had approaching Warne to be part of the infamous match-fixing regime.

Warne had refused point blank and when Pakistan won the first Test by one wicket in a thrilling finish at Karachi, Salim on the victory rostrum had hissed to Warne: "You should have taken the money!"

From that day on the Australians dubbed Salim "The Rat" and never spoke or even acknowledged him, not even at practice. Along with another who had caved in to the bookmakers, India's Mohammad Azharuddin, he was to be run out of cricket.

Continuing what was to become a long-term love affair with the 'Gabba, Warne amassed 11 wickets for the match, including an extraordinary seven for 23 from just 16 overs in the first innings in conditions more beneficial for the faster bowlers. In one extraordinary spell he took 6-10 from 56 balls. He was again Man of the Match, the Pakistanis surrendering so meekly that ex-Testman Jeff Thomson referred to the tourists as a "Z" grade pub team.

SCOREBOARD: *Australia 463 (S.R. Waugh 112 not out) defeated Pakistan 97 (S.K. Warne 16.1-9-23-7) and 240 (S.K. Warne 27.5-10-54-4) by an innings and 126 runs. Warne Test No.39*

8. NOVEMBER, 1996: 2nd TEST v WEST INDIES, Sydney

A stunning counter-attacking 71 by West Indian left-hander Shivnarine Chanderpaul gave the West Indies a scent of victory on the fifth morning. Two balls before lunch, Warne landed a leg-break wide on the return crease. As Chanderpaul went to play a forcing shot, it turned at right angles to strike his middle and off stumps, a pumped-up Warne celebrating with two clenched fists. It was another one of those amazing-but-true deliveries Warne was to be renowned for throughout his career. And once again Australia was on the road to victory.

"It was as unplayable a ball as you could get," said wicketkeeper Ian Healy.

SCOREBOARD: *Australia 331 (C.A. Walsh 5-98) and 4-312 dec. defeated West Indies 304 (S.K. Warne 35.2-13-65-3) and 215 (S.K. Warne 27.4-5-95-4) by 124 runs. Warne Test No.46*

9. JULY, 1997: 3rd TEST v ENGLAND, Manchester

For the first time in 10 years, Australia had conceded the early lead and any hopes of an Ashes squaring victory ended with the

London rains which spoiled the second Test.

Ignoring the advice of his team's faster bowlers, Mark Taylor won the toss and batted. It was a green seamer and the bowlers would have been delighted to have fielded first.

Steve Waugh scored two priceless hundreds and Warne, who had been a little out of sorts returned to his devastating best, despite one flipper which soared head-high past a retreating Andy Caddick's nose. He took wickets in his 7th, 11th, 13th, 15th, 19th and 29th overs as Australia easily defended a modest first innings score.

Set 469, England succumbed a second time for only 200, Warne taking three key wickets including Alec Stewart (1) and Graham Thorpe (7). On a bare, turning wicket which prompted Ian Healy to don a helmet for one of the few times in his career, Warne's accuracy was phenomenal. The Englishmen were eventually strangled into stagnation before submitting totally. "The slumbering giant was aroused," said the *Wisden* reporter.

During the game, Warne passed Richie Benaud's 248 Test wickets to become Australia's greatest ever wicket-taking leg-spinner ... it had taken him seven years and 56 Tests, compared with Benaud's 248 in 13 years and 63 Tests.

Afterwards Warne, pumped and at his cavalier best, cavorted on the balcony, wiggling his hips, swigging from a bottle of champagne and directing one-fingered salutes at hecklers in the crowd. The picture made back pages around the world. All in all it had been a most satisfying day.

SCOREBOARD: *Australia 235 (S.R. Waugh 108) and 8-395 dec. (S.R. Waugh 116) defeated England 162 (S.K. Warne 30-14-48-6) and 200 (30.4-8-63-3) by 268 runs. Warne Test No. 56*

10. JANUARY, 1998: 2nd TEST v SOUTH AFRICA, Sydney

At the end of a rainy Sydney day after most of the crowd had gone home and *A Current Affair* had replaced the cricket on the box, Warne clean bowled Jacques Kallis with a top-spinner to claim his 300th Test scalp. So sure was Kallis that it was the leg-break that he offered no shot. "The sight of a bemused Kallis, minus his bails and an exultant bowler with arms aloft, leaning backwards as the boys raced in to smother him, was Warnie at his theatrical best," wrote Steve Waugh later. "The guy is a genius, the Kasparov of cricket, always thinking one step ahead."

Warne was irrepressible with 11 wickets for the match. No other Australian spinner had made the 300 wickets milestone. His coach, Terry Jenner, ventured that he could double it before he finished. Australia's win secured the series and the World Test Championship. Warne was Man of the Match and his dual helicopter arm celebrations totally appropriate.

SCOREBOARD: *Australia 421 (M.E. Waugh 100) defeated South Africa 287 (S.K. Warne 32.1-8-75-5) and 113 (S.K. Warne 21-9-34-6) by an innings and 21 runs. Warne Test No.63*

11. MARCH, 2000: 2nd TEST v NEW ZEALAND, Wellington

A serious shoulder injury and the low and slow Indian wickets had curtailed Warne's progress for several seasons. But in this engrossing Test, the highlight of the most entertaining trans-Tasman series of all time, Warne showed he was back to his dominant and destructive best.

In the Test after he broke Dennis Lillee's Australian record tally of 355 wickets Warne's match return of 7-160 was emphatic and included a trademark flipper which castled Nathan Astle. Australia won a ninth successive match, breaking the 79-year-old record held by Warwick Armstrong's team for most winning Tests in a row.

SCOREBOARD: *Australia 419 (M.J. Slater 143, S.R. Waugh 151 not out) and 4-177 defeated New Zealand 298 (C.L. Cairns 109 S.K. Warne 14.5-1-65-4) and 294 (S.K. Warne 27-7-92-3) by six wickets. Warne Test No.83*

Photo: Cricket Victoria

12. AUGUST, 2001: 3rd TEST v ENGLAND, Nottingham

Wisden reported that "Warne truly turned the Test on its head." In a gripping, low-scoring affair, he effectively clinched the Ashes by precipitating England's collapse from 2-115 to 162 all out.

Warne was at his dominating and dictating best. "Come on Ramps, you know you want to," he called to English batsman Mark Ramprakash near the close of the second day. Within moments, Ramprakash (on 26) had charged Warne, missed and been stumped by a metre.

The psychological dominance was complete. Once again Warne was Man of the Match.

SCOREBOARD: *Australia 190 (A.J. Tudor 5-44) and 3-158 defeated England 185 (G.D. McGrath 5-49, S.K. Warne 16-4-37-2) and 162 (S.K. Warne 18-5-33-6) by 7 wickets. Warne Test No.91*

13. AUGUST, 2001: 5th TEST v ENGLAND, London (The Oval)

Wicket No.400, among 11 for the match, a couple of slips catches including the matchwinner, a huge victory to sew up the series 4-1 and another Man of the Match award. And all this at the end of a tiring tour, on a pitch tailor-made for batsmen!

"Aussie Alec" Stewart became Warne's 400th milestone victim when caught behind off a big leggie in the first innings. It was also Stewart who was the victim of a brilliant over in the second innings. Like a rabbit blinded by headlights, he was eventually bowled, without offering a shot to a spitting delivery from around the wicket which spun straight across him.

SCOREBOARD: *Australia 4-641 dec. (J.L. Langer 102 not out, M.E. Waugh 120, S.R. Waugh 157 not out) defeated England 432 (M.R. Ramprakash 133, S.K. Warne 44.2-7-165-7) and 184 (G.D. McGrath 5-43, S.K. Warne 28-8-64-4) by an innings and 25 runs. Warne Test No.92*

14. DECEMBER, 2001: 1st TEST v SOUTH AFRICA, Adelaide

South Africa was billed as being legitimate challengers for Australia's position as the world's outstanding Test nation. But single-handedly Warne showed they were not even in the race. He maintained premium pressure throughout, sending down 70 overs. On the fourth evening, Warne was introduced in the fourth over of the South African second innings. After a dropped catch from his first ball, Gary Kirsten was caught at silly point from the last ball of the day. South Africa was 2-17 and there was no way back. Warne was named Man of the Match.

SCOREBOARD: *Australia 439 (D.R. Martyn 124 not out, J.L. Langer 116) and 7-309 dec. (M.L. Hayden 131) defeated South Africa 374 (S.K. Warne 39.4-9-113-5) and 128 (S.K. Warne 29-7-57-3) by 246 runs. Warne Test No.96*

15. MARCH, 2002: 2nd TEST v SOUTH AFRICA, Cape Town

Benefiting from a diet and fitness regime, Warne conjured up more magic in his 100th Test. An exhaustive schedule was beginning to take a toll on bodies. Warne summoned up all his reserves to bowl nearly 100 overs.

South Africa, bouncing back from a sequence of humiliations, were competitive without mastering the leg-spinner. The last five South African second innings wickets fell for 42 to keep Australia's run chase within reach. Eight wickets and a vital innings of 63 guaranteed Man of the Match honours.

Afterwards, Steve Waugh, his captain wrote:"Warnie, as we all know and have seen once again, is a genius, a once-in-a-lifetime phenomenon ... he turned in a colossal effort. Without his stamina and consistency, we would have struggled to bowl South Africa out."

SCOREBOARD: *Australia 382 (A.C. Gilchrist 138) and 6-334 (R.T. Ponting 100 not out) defeated South Africa 239 (S.K. Warne 28-10-70-2) and 473 (S.K. Warne 70-15-161-6) by four wickets. Warne Test No.100*

16. OCTOBER, 2002: 1st TEST v PAKISTAN, Colombo

In this "on the road" Test series against Pakistan, Warne saved Australia from a surprise defeat at Colombo's Sara Stadium. The batsmen faltered against Shoaib Akhtar's pace, but Warne's 11 wicket match haul was the decisive counter.

He took seven in the first innings, broke the dangerous Pakistani opening partnership in the second innings and also trapped in-form Younis Khan (51) at a crucial time. Warne became the only Australian cricketer to be named Man of the Match having scored a pair.

SCOREBOARD: *Australia 467 (R.T. Ponting 141) and 127 (Shoaib Akhtar 5-21) defeated Pakistan 279 (S.K. Warne 24.3-7-94-7) and 274 (S.K. Warne 30.3-3.94-4) by 41 runs. Warne Test No.102*

17. OCTOBER, 2002: 3rd TEST v PAKISTAN, Sharjah (U.A.E.)

From the extreme humidity of Colombo to the boiling temperatures of Sharjah there was no stopping the champion. The ground was empty, the heat unbearable and the series already won. But Warne was indefatigable and collected eight more wickets to finish with 27 for the three games. He made inroads into the top order and made short work of the tail. It was "vintage" Warnie. Another Man of the Match award resulted.

SCOREBOARD: *Australia 444 (R.T. Ponting 150, S.R. Waugh 103 not out) defeated Pakistan 221 (S.K. Warne 30.1-10-74-5) and 203 (S.K. Warne 21-3-56-3) by an innings and 20 runs. Warne Test No.104*

18. NOVEMBER, 2002: 2nd TEST v ENGLAND, Adelaide

Twice in this Test England threatened to re-take the momentum. In the first innings they reached 3-295. Then Warne and Jason Gillespie took the last seven wickets for 47. In the second innings, rain offered England the chance of a draw. Warne tied down England's No.1 batsman Michael Vaughan before having him wonderfully caught at deep square leg by a diving Glenn McGrath. The Test was soon over and another successful Ashes defence assured.

SCOREBOARD: *Australia 9-552 dec. (R.T. Ponting 154) defeated England 342 (M.P. Vaughan 177, S.K. Warne 34-10-93-4) and 159 (S.K. Warne 25-7-36-3) by an innings and 51 runs. Warne Test No.106*

19. MARCH, 2004: 1st TEST v SRI LANKA, Galle

Returning after his 12-month suspension, Warne was thrown straight into a tough series in the country of his main rival for the title of the world's best spinner.

In a fairytale return, the Australian took 10 wickets and Muthiah Muralidaran 11, but it was Australia who came from behind to complete a magnificent victory in Ricky Ponting's first Test as captain. Additionally, Warne beat Murali to the 500th wicket milestone when he captured the vital scalp of Hashan Tillakaratne. The top-edged sweep held by debutant Andrew Symonds sewed up the win and assured for Warne the Man of the Match.

"Things in my life have always been a drama, so today leaves me very happy and proud," Warne said.

SCOREBOARD: *Australia 220 (M. Muralidaran 6-59) and 9-512 dec. (M.L. Hayden 130, D.S. Lehmann 129, D.R. Martyn 110, M. Muralidaran 5-153) defeated Sri Lanka 381 (T.M. Dilshan 104, S.K. Warne 42.4-9-116-5) and 154 (S.K. Warne 15-5-43-5) by 197 runs. Warne Test No.108*

Right: Trent Bridge, 1997: More Pommy scalps

20. MARCH, 2004: 2nd TEST v SRI LANKA, Kandy

An even more thrilling Test and another wonderful 10-wicket performance gave Warne more Man of the Match honours at the home town of his great rival "Murali". Sri Lanka began the last day needing just 51 runs to win with three wickets standing. Three times Chaminda Vaas sent the ball to the boundary. Going for a fourth boundary he was caught off guess-who. Warne had once again turned a match.

SCOREBOARD: *Australia 120 and 442 (D.R. Martyn 161, A.C. Gilchrist 144, M. Muralidaran 5-173) defeated Sri Lanka 211 (S.K. Warne 20.1-3-65-5) and 324 (S.T. Jayasuriya 131, S.K. Warne 21.1-2-90-5) by 27 runs. Warne Test No.109*

21. NOVEMBER, 2004: 1st TEST v NEW ZEALAND, Brisbane

Back at his favorite 'Gabba, Warne turned New Zealand inside out after they had begun the opening Test of the series strongly. Warne first kept them in check and then on the Sunday afternoon ripped their second innings apart. Once first innings century maker, giant left-hander Jacob Oram was caught by Matthew Hayden, an early finish was inevitable.

SCOREBOARD: *Australia 585 (M.J. Clarke 141, A.C. Gilchrist 126, C.S. Martin 5-152) defeated New Zealand 353 (J.D.P. Oram 126 not out, S.K. Warne 29.3-3-97-4) and 76 (S.K. Warne 10.2-3-15-4) by an innings and 156 runs. Warne Test No.116*

22. NOVEMBER, 2005: 3rd TEST V WEST INDIES, Adelaide

Brian Lara's fantastic Aussie farewell double century and surpassing of the all-time Test run aggregate was the feature of an excellent match. But in the end, even the Trinidadian master had to give way to Warne. The leg-spinner once more grabbed the initiative for Australia in a Test hanging in the balance.

Australia led by just 23 runs on the first innings and had to bat last. Warne, though, was brilliant on an Adelaide pitch which had begun to wear. He had Lara cheaply and stunningly taken by Hayden at slip in the second innings and from there totally eroded the confidence of the brittle West Indian side.

SCOREBOARD: *Australia 428 (M.E.K. Hussey 133 not out, D.J. Bravo 6-84) and 3-182 defeated the West Indies 405 (B.C. Lara 226, S.K. Warne 19.2-2-77-1) and 204 (S.K. Warne 33-9-80-6) by seven wickets. Warne Test No.131*

23. MARCH, 2006: 2nd TEST v SOUTH AFRICA, Durban

While teams like India, the West Indies and Sri Lanka at times did well against Warne, the South Africans never ever truly mastered him. The series of 2005-06 was a case in point, the longer the game going the better Warne becoming.

On a seamer's wicket, he bowled out the Proteas on the last day. Significantly, that included South Africa's No.1 player Jacques Kallis for seven, lbw trying to sweep.

Warne was named Man of the Match in a game in which his captain made twin centuries.

SCOREBOARD: *Australia 369 (R.T. Ponting 103) and 4-307 dec. (R.T. Ponting 116, M.L. Hayden 102) defeated South Africa 267 (J.H. Kallis 114, B. Lee 5-69, S.K. Warne 25-2-80-2) and 297 (S.K. Warne 35.5-9-86-6) by 112 runs. Warne Test No.137*

24. DECEMBER, 2006: 2nd TEST v ENGLAND, Adelaide

In the greatest 'it ain't over till it's over' performance of them all Warne inspired Australia to a wonderful last day Ashes victory. Statistically, he had bowled better and turned the ball more. But in

terms of exerting pressure and influence over the opposition this was the granddaddy of all.

The game had been meandering to a draw, so it seemed, before England shut up shop and refused to play shots on the last day. Warne circled and then struck, again and again. When the super-confident Kevin Pietersen was bowled behind his legs, an unlikely win beckoned, Australia adopting limited-over type aggression to secure the match with just minutes to spare. Afterwards England's Steve Harmison said: "I sensed the Australians were as disbelieving as we were over the result."

Justin Langer said Warne's success was especially satisfying as England's coach Duncan Fletcher had suggested his batsmen finally had Warnie's measure. "Today, Warnie entertained the world with pure competitive genius ... the difference between the awesome successes of the team compared with others lies often in the brilliance of Warnie."

SCOREBOARD: *Australia 513 (R.T. Ponting 142, M.J. Clarke 124, M.J. Hoggard 7-109) and 4-168 defeated England 6-551 dec. (P.D. Collingwood 206, K.P. Pietersen 158, S.K. Warne 53-9-167-1) and 129 (S.K. Warne 32-12-49-4) by six wickets. Warne Test No.142*

25. DECEMBER, 2006: 4th TEST v ENGLAND, Melbourne

In the euphoria of Warne taking his 700th Test wicket in front of almost 90,000 at the MCG on Boxing Day just days after announcing his impending retirement from Test cricket, his skill in bowling out England on the first day on a pitch suited to quicks is easily forgotten.

The ball did not turn a long way, but the master of flight, guile and variation yorked Andrew Strauss for the 700th and did a mini lap of honour to the delight of celebrating Melburnians.

Pietersen, England's No. 1 batsman, was induced into a big hitting indiscretion before Warne tormented the tail to be Man of the Match on his Melbourne farewell.

SCOREBOARD: *Australia 419 (A. Symonds 156, M.L. Hayden 153) defeated England 159 (S.K. Warne 17.2-4-39-5) and 161 (S.K. Warne 19-3-46-2) by an innings and 99 runs. Warne Test No. 144*

AND ONE WHICH GOT AWAY
SEPTEMBER-OCTOBER, 1994: 1st Test v PAKISTAN, Karachi

Australia was on the verge of a historic win in Karachi, the citadel of Pakistani cricket. With eight wickets for the game, Warne had again been super-charged as he mowed through Pakistan's middle-order.

But there was revival and from 9-258, needing 314, Inzamam-el-Haq and No.11 Mushtaq Ahmed shared an inspired last wicket stand which was to snatch a remarkable one-wicket victory.

"We needed three to win and Inzamam tried to whip Shane Warne through mid-wicket against the spin," said "Mushie". "Warnie was at the top of his game and he spun the ball square. Inzi lost his balance, stumbled out of his crease and fell over as the ball went past him and the stumps. Ian Healy failed to gather and so missed one of the easiest stumpings ever. I never thought he would miss one like this. It went through his arms and legs and we ran three byes to win the Test, Healy sank to the ground and could not get up for about 10 minutes. One of the Aussies told me that they had to pick him up and lead him from the pitch to the dressing room."

The Australian version was that the ball had grubbed along the ground, flicked Inzi's pad and just missed everything.

They were amazed Mushtaq (20 not out) had stayed so long. Previously he'd hardly been able to hit the spinners off the square.

"It wasn't an easy stumping," said Heals, "but I should have made it, especially in that pressure situation. The Queenslander kicked over the stumps in his fury. It was one which got away.

SCOREBOARD: *Pakistan 256 (S.K. Warne 27-10-61-3) and 9-315 (S.K. Warne 36.1-12-89-5) defeated Australia 337 and 232 (D.C. Boon 114 not out) by one wicket. Warne Test No. 27*

QUOTES

"He is a genius. It is a privilege to watch someone like him."
ARCHBISHOP DESMOND TUTU

"He is the king. The best bowler ever."
JUSTIN LANGER

"Shane Warne is a gentleman, one of the most honest and generous blokes that I know. All the success that he has had, the fabulous contracts he has attracted – he has earned and deserved every single one of them."
DAVID BOON

"Shane Warne came into the Australian team just at the right time, as far as my career was concerned ... in the seasons that followed I was lucky to have the best seat in the house ... as Warnie decimated opposition batting line-ups the world over and changed the way international cricket looked at its spin bowlers."
IAN HEALY

"Shane is a living legend. He is the most intelligent and talented leg spinner that I have ever seen or am likely to see in my life. He is a proud man and a brilliant guy. He also bats a bit and is a superb slip fielder."
MUSHTAQ AHMED

"To me Shane is the best bowler. I have bowled leg spin and I know how hard it is. Your shoulder has to rotate more and so for Shane to survive for as long as he did was a tribute to his stamina and ability."
MUTHIAH MURALIDARAN

Brain Snaps, Bans And Broadsides

Moments even a wayward son would love to have back again, from Jo'burg to Colombo ...

Australian cricketers on tour are feted like movie stars. Everything is laid on: swish hotels, fashionable restaurants, drink cards, gambling money, the lot. It's a fantastic lifestyle.

When Shane Warne arrived at Johannesburg's Jan Smuts Airport in February, 2004, he and all the Australians were stunned by their reception. This was the first official Australian visit for a fair dinkum Test series in almost 25 years and it seemed half the city had turned out, black and white.

The team was besieged. Hundreds of autograph hunters flocked around Warne, still bathing in the glory of *that ball* and his fresh status as cricket's hottest new celebrity.

Bodyguards were hired to control the throngs but for weeks he was confronted, in hotel foyers, at dinner tables, everywhere. He was the Sultan of Spin, the new Wizard of Oz. Everyone wanted a slice.

On the field, too, he was targeted by aggressive crowds, some of whom threw missiles. He was called a wanker and sworn at. Much of the abuse was delivered in Afrikaans, but there was no mistaking the venom.

Further darkening his mood was the cavalier treatment of his bowling by South Africa's golden boy Hansie Cronje who in the game before the first Test made 251 and declared Warne easy-meat.

Warne was clearly affected by it all and come the first Test at Johannesburg's Bullring, South Africa's premier cricket venue, he snapped, abusing local opener Andrew Hudson with, "#@^%-0off, go on Hudson, #@^%-0off outta here", after he had dismissed him third ball.

I'd hired him as a celebrity columnist for the Australian *Cricketer*, the magazine I edited for 15 years and he'd expressed his remorse, saying, "for a few seconds, I lost control of myself and now I will have to work hard to repair the damage".

It was a violent attack, totally alien to the spirit of the game

> **"#@^%-0off.**
> **Go on Hudson.**
> **#@^%-0off**
> **outta here"**

and impossible to ignore, even if Warne was still smarting after earlier being struck by an orange while fielding. Hudson, a church-on-Sundays-man, shook his head in amazement as Warne continued to vent his fury, even when being held back by his teammates. Umpire David Shepherd, as kindly a soul as you could ever meet, was equally stunned and immediately called Allan Border over to restore order.

A heavy fine resulted amid a huge media backlash. Captain-to-be Mark Taylor also delivered an in-between Tests lecture, reminding Warne of some of the responsibilities that went with being a member of Australia's elite cricket team.

In his bid to be aggressive, always part of his bowling persona, Warne admitted he'd had a brain snap and brought the game into disrepute. His sledging of Hudson, however, wasn't an aberration, a totally out-of-character incident to be treated in isolation. He'd been

strutting and tormenting ever since his school days at Mentone Grammar. It was part of his persona. He had the healthiest of respects for his own ability and if he could also distract a batsman enough for them to make an error, well and good. Captains, grateful for his winning ways, had for years turned a blind eye to it all.

Only weeks before the Hudson outburst, Warne had borrowed some of teammate Merv Hughes' bristle and abused another South African, Daryll Cullinan, tit-for-tat, he said, after Cullinan had sledged him over his weight.

"Leave some lunch for us, Fatso," Warne claimed Cullinan had said when he came into bat shortly before an interval.

"He'd been in Test cricket five minutes and he's carrying on like this," said Warne in his autobiography.

It was a preamble to Warne's coarse send-off of Cullinan ("#@^%-0off") which triggered ACB chairman Alan Crompton to issue a statement saying such behaviour was "cowardly and un-Australian" and totally alien to the morals of the game. In future there would be zero tolerance.

Just five weeks later Warne over-stepped and paid heavily for a moment he'd love to have back again. But his on-field banter and broadsides were to continue as he became the cornerstone and ultimate match-winner in the most intimidating cricket team of all.

The Australians were at a beachside casino in Colombo, having some down-time during an autumn tournament in 1994 when Warne inadvertently stepped into an embarrassing no-man's land which was to see his name linked with three who infamously sold the game out: Hansie Cronje, Salim Malik and Mohammad Azharuddin.

Warne was on a downer. Red 23 wasn't proving as lucky as usual and despite his ability to "count" and know the various percentages, he'd lost thousands when teammate Mark Waugh introduced him to a man called "John", who he said was from India. Waugh said John was a great fan of Shane's and that he bet on the cricket.

The following night John invited Warnie to his room and as a token of his admiration handed him an envelope containing $US5000 in greenbacks to "go and have some fun with".

There were positively no strings, he said, and he'd be personally affronted if Warne didn't accept. After hesitating initially, Warne took the money and high-rolled it back at the casino.

Less than three months later the phone calls started, John wishing Warne and his family Merry Christmas and asking the first of many questions about weather and pitch conditions.

Waugh was also on John's payroll and he, too, provided information on a regular basis. When quizzed in the New Year by Australia's team manager Ian McDonald, Waugh said it was money for jam.

All the other Australians, too, were interviewed on a one-on-one basis, captain Mark Taylor camped in a back room listening. Chief executive Graham Halbish had suspected if anyone was involved it was likely to be Waugh and Warne, but he, Taylor and McDonald were still amazed by the admissions. They couldn't believe how stupid the pair had been. The Board had been leading the charge against corruption in cricket and this was an untimely, unfathomable embarrassment.

One option was to immediately have the errant pair disciplined and sent home from the West Indies, but rather than being transparent and making a full admission - a press release had already been prepared in anticipation - the Board opted to stay silent and hope the issue could remain in-house.

Privately, they handed out the biggest solo fines in cricket history and according to Halbish "put the fear of God" into the pair.

The scandal went unreported for four years but when it was uncovered, by *The Australian*'s Malcolm Conn, and it was found Warne as well as Mark Waugh had been involved, all hell broke loose.

*T*here is a price for fame and sometimes, just sometimes, Shane Warne would like to be Shane nobody, able to go to the park or the pictures with his loved ones without being pestered.

Tourist buses would stop outside his Brighton mansion and up to 40 would claw for position at his steel picket gates, hoping he might be in his front garden and agree to a chat or a happy snap.

It put enormous stress and scrutiny on his private life, strain which anyone would have found intolerable.

Wherever cricket's human headline went – England, South Africa or the West Indies - it seemed he was more often making the front pages rather than the sports sections.

The Fleet Street tabloids had a field day at his expense, some trying to set him up by sending call girls to his room and having them kiss-and-tell. He made almost as many banners as Princess Diana.

Back home in Melbourne, the top-selling *New Idea* published a story by a stripper who had claimed to have had a three-month affair with Warne after they met at a lap-dancing club. MY WILD NIGHTS WITH SHANE was the headline. Later the stripper's husband said he'd love to get physical with Warne.

During the '99 tour of the Caribbean, Warne was photographed dragging on a cigarette despite having a $200,000 contract to desist

from Nicorette. In Bridgetown, we were out to tea and just happened to walk into the same restaurant bar as the Australians. While most were camped in little groups out in the back beer garden, Warne was up the front of the bar perched on a stool. Alongside him was a pretty West Indian girl, her hair beautifully braided, seemingly hanging on his every word. He saw us and nodded a hello as we shimmied past into the back restaurant. My wife Susan said to me: "Wasn't that Shane Warne?"

*N*o-one can divide opinion quite like Shane Warne and unknowingly, he almost caused a punch-up one otherwise inconsequential afternoon in the WACA press box.

The heat had been turned up on Warne over Scott Muller, the Queensland fast bowler who came and went as fast as he'd arrived.

Warne had been bowling in a Test in Hobart (1999-2000) when a voice was picked up via the stumps microphone: "Can't bowl, can't throw."

Muller had shown himself to be a class short of Test cricket and at least someone knew it – and said so.

Being closest to the nearest mike, Warne was immediately blamed. Newspaper editors with an anti-Warne bias went into overdrive, instructing their writers to dig deep.

Warne proclaimed his innocence and even called Muller to say so, but the Queenslander was unconvinced, the conversation ending with an abrupt "#@^%-0off". When Muller took a wicket in an interstate game he walked past the stumps and yelled into the microphone: "How was that one Warnie!"

The heat was just as intense in the press box. Warne's critics wanted to believe that it was him and not Joe Previtera, the Channel

9 cameraman who claimed responsibility, saying his microphone had inadvertently been in the on position.

A week later in the WACA press box, when *The Australian*'s Malcolm Conn called for an impromptu count of hands of those who thought Warne hadn't said it, only one was raised, that of *The Age*'s Martin Blake.

"You're a goose," said Conn to his old mate.

The normally easygoing Blake lost his cool, knocked over a chair and went at Conn, grabbing him around the neck and snapping a chain which held his press pass.

Holding a clenched fist just inches from Conn's nose, Blake said: "Don't ever call me a goose."

Later after more investigations it was found, once and for all, that Warne hadn't been lying. The voice wasn't his. Conn and Blake made up that very night over a beer. And Warnie? He thought it was hilarious.

*F*ew sportsmen have shared Warnie's habit for headlines, but at least some of it was self-imposed.

Take his drug bust on the eve of the 2003 World Cup in South Africa which saw him suspended for 12 months. Initially he announced a challenge, but backed off after learning that he risked a doubling of his ban which may have finished his career entirely.

His mother, Brigitte, had given him some of her slimming pills before a TV interview and "Vain Shane", as he was dubbed, took them without a second thought.

As in Colombo when a shady character he didn't know had offered a brown bag of money, warning bells should have rung - but they didn't. The diuretic tablets were on sport's banned list. They'd been used by others as a masking agent for performance-

enhancers.

Captain Ricky Ponting said Warne was merely a victim of his own vanity, but he'd also been naive and stupid and given the importance of the World Cup, let his teammates down. Badly.

The Australians had been lectured about the need to be absolutely sure about any tablets they took. "If in doubt, ring "Hooter" (the team's long-time physiotherapist and Jack-of-all-trades Errol Alcott)," they were told.

Warne said it was like being back at school again. He hadn't bothered listening. He was never to play another one-day game for Australia again. The likeable larrikin had put his foot in it. Again. Like never before.

A Soapie Star

"Warne is a millionaire larrikin. More like a soapie star... that's why is success is as likely topolarise opinion rather than unify it in celebration,"
The Bulletin's MAX WALSH

1995 Australians in the Caribbean

"I don't think I'm a rebel – I've got a lot of old-fashioned traits,"
SHANE WARNE

"What on earth got into Shane Warne in the first Test in Johannesburg? ... I read somewhere that Warne said he had been possessed by demons. Well in that case I'm a Dutchman,"
IAN BOTHAM

"Under pressure he turns into a boor. The pleasant young man of television interviews is readily interchangeable with an immature hothead,"
Melbourne journalist PATRICK SMITH

"We fined the two players (Warne and Waugh) heavily and put the fear of God into them. They knew if there was ever a sniff of them being involved in anything similar again, their careers would surely end,"
Australian cricket administrator GRAHAM HALBISH

"A certain percentage of the public out there just don't like you for whatever reason; they're jealous of you; they just don't like the way you conduct yourself or the way you play. They think you're arrogant. All you can do is be yourself,"
SHANE WARNE

Regrets ... I've Had A Few

Warnie remains the best captain Australia never had

When Shane Warne was Australia's one-day captain he did it with flair and imagination. He was animated, entertaining and deeply involved. He loved the role. Allan Border and Ian Chappell thought him a breath of fresh air, teammates like Paul Reiffel spoke of his magnetism and sheer inspiration.

In winning 10 of his 11 games standing-in for Steve Waugh, Warne re-opened the debate about whether bowlers could also be successful captains in the fiercer and more demanding cauldron of Test cricket.

The last bowler to toss the coin for the Aussies had been Rodney Hogg, and that was only a one-off when Allan Border was indisposed in the lead-up to a one-dayer in Melbourne.

Warnie desperately wanted the job. He regarded it as the ultimate accolade.

Despite shoulder surgery and the complications triggered by his unwitting involvement in the bookmaking scandal, he'd just become Australia's greatest-ever Test wicket taker and in the public arena, anyway, he was very much The Prodigal Son.

When Waugh went down spectacularly in a Test in Kandy, Warne had led passionately and lifted the Australians, coming from a long way back.

They may have lost the Test but it was noticeable how the players rallied around Warne. There was an extra, emotional edge to their cricket, a little like the World Cup semi-final at Edgbaston in '99 when he turned the match on its head with three for none in eight balls.

Minutes before taking the field, he'd told his teammates that he intended to retire if the Australians lost. His opening volleys were spectacular, South African Herschelle Gibbs falling second ball with a delivery reminiscent of *that ball* which castled Mike Gatting at Old Trafford six years earlier. 'YEAH.... COME ONNNN!!!' yelled Warne, pumping his fist in the air after bowling the drifting, spitting gem-of-a-delivery. Once again he'd affected a game as only he could.

"Shane was so fired up and animated that it took a wall of players to stifle his forward thrust (celebration)," wrote Waugh in his autobiography. "His drive and will were literally scary but it sparked life into others who were tensing up under the South African onslaught and it got us back into the game."

Wicketkeeper Adam Gilchrist said the delivery was simply unplayable and the best ball he'd ever kept to. "I had the best seat in the house to observe that delivery," he said. "Luckily it hit the off stump because it was on its way for four byes if it had missed! (It turned so far that Gilchrist initially moved with the drift down the leg side)."

Thanks to Warne's counter-attack, the Australians defended a modest total and in a thrilling finale, forced a tie. It was good enough to lift them into the final and they duly won that, too, Warne later being talked out of retirement by family and friends.

But storm clouds were brewing, not only for Warne, but for the game itself with accusations of greedy players on the take, including the captain of South Africa, pin-up boy Hansie Cronje.

Warne's cricket credentials were impeccable, but his regular frontpage appearances in the London tabloids and his sensational involvement with "John" the bookmaker, first made public in 1998-99, four years after the event, had irretrievably affected his standing with some of those in Mahogany Row. They couldn't understand how stupid he and Mark Waugh had been in encouraging such a dangerous liaison.

A series of off-field dramas with women followed, including a particularly damaging one involving a pretty married girl 10 years his junior, Donna Wright.

She accused him of sexual harassment via a string of lurid mobile phone messages.

Warne defended himself on *A Current Affair,* claiming the story had been distorted. He didn't know how his hotel room key had finished in Ms Wright's back pocket. He agreed there had been some "dirty talk" but he had merely been reciprocating. He gave the impression that he had been set-up, but he was unconvincing.

> *"... Warnie desperately wanted the job. He regarded it as the ultimate accolade."*

Asked by Channel Nine's Mike Munro if he felt this latest scandal could irretrievably finish his captaincy aspirations, he said he hoped not, that this was a private matter and it was disappointing it had been made public. Not once did he offer an apology. For many of us watching from afar it seemed to be a PR opportunity wasted. "Okay," he could have said, "I stuffed up, but let's all get on with life...."

Warnie might have been a genius of a cricketer, a once-in-a-

lifetime player, but captains of Australia needed to be white knights and ambassadors. They couldn't afford to act so injudiciously. Warnie lived for the moment with few cares. Those on the Board who may have been wavering in their judgments now knew that Warne was too much of a headliner, too unpredictable and too flamboyant a character for such a high office.

Eighteen months earlier, rather than going with a high spirited wildcard, they had opted to go a less complicated, safer route and selected Waugh as Test and one-day captain. They had been shown to be right and any chance Warne had of again seriously challenging dissipated with the Donna Wright Affair, which was played out endlessly in all the English tabloids in the summer of 2000.

The Board acted promptly back home, voting unanimously to replace Warne as vice-captain. As Waugh termed it, Warnie had finally used all of his "get-out-of-jail" cards.

He was to remain an inspirational on-field force, a champion foot soldier, whose match-winning ways rivalled and even surpassed those of Don Bradman.

But he was never again to be in contention for the captaincy.

And his marriage … it was fast heading for the rocks.

Australia's Most Successful ODI Captains

	Mts*	Wins	Strike-rate
1. Shane Warne	11	10	90%
2. Ricky Ponting	148	115	77%
3. Adam Gilchrist	15	11	73%
4. Steve Waugh	106	67	63%
5. Allan Border	178	107	60%
6. Ian Chappell	11	6	54%
7. Mark Taylor	67	36	53%
8. Greg Chappell	49	21	42%
9. Kim Hughes	49	21	42%

*Minimum 10 games

QUOTES

"He left messages saying the most disgusting things I have ever heard. It was perverted. It made me sick in the stomach." nurse DONNA WRIGHT

"It's fair to say he (Warne) put himself in an embarrassing position in regards to his personal life, public perceptions of him and the aspirations of the ACB."
Australian Cricket Board chief executive MALCOLM SPEED

"I couldn't believe it was happening. It was a mistake, yes, but it was a private matter and had nothing to do with cricket. Explicit talk on the telephone did not mean all of a sudden I'd lost my flipper or had forgotten how to set a field." SHANE WARNE

"The initial press conference (in India) was a little strange without Warnie (alongside) who during the 2000 off-season had used all his 'get-out-of-jail' cards with the board and been replaced by Adam Gilchrist as vice-captain."
STEVE WAUGH

"No, he shouldn't have been Test captain.
He was an extremely good tactician and intuitive and
a leader. However, there were other times when his
emotions would get the better of him, be it due to him
not performing to the exceptional standards he set for
himself, or due to certain personal reasons.
As captain, one of the important traits of leadership is to
remain consistent, irrespective of personal performance
or off-field complications. For Shane to perform on
his stage, the cricket arena, he needed to arrive at the
ground 'fresh and relaxed'.
In his own words, this may require him to stay up late at
night to clear anything from his mind. Once he felt that
was all sorted and he could relax, he was able to then
compartmentalise his game and away he went. He was a
champion once he crossed the line."

Long-time Australian coach JOHN BUCHANAN

"Warnie did a brilliant job (as a first-time
captain of Australia), full of invention and challenges.
True to Warnie, almost everything came off, even when
remonstrating with the MCG fans who were belting us
(English) fielders with golf and billiard balls.
Ever the showman he borrowed Mark Waugh's helmet
before pleading with the culprits (to stop). They did.
The man's a genius."

DARREN GOUGH

Warnie v The Don

Warnie won more Tests for Australia than even Don Bradman

*W*hen Shane Warne was a star-struck rookie, wondering if he truly deserved to be in the same dressing room alongside heroes and icons like Allan Border, he told me how all he really wanted to do was take a timely wicket which changed the match momentum and helped his team win.

His concentration was always towards the team, a key reason why he was so loved by his teammates and adored by the public.

I was sitting with a good friend Graham Wilson, the guitar player from The Four Kinsmen, on the balcony seats of the old Cigar Stand at the MCG in 1992 when Warnie surprised Richie Richardson with his scuttling flipper which hit the base of middle and off. For a life-long cricket fan like Graham, he said it was almost as memorable a moment as when the Kinsmen won the first of a fleet of Mo awards for being Australia's leading entertainers.

We all jumped with Warnie. It was a key wicket just as the world champion Windies were threatening to take control. Warnie had turned his first Test in Australia and in front of his home town crowd. He was ecstatic. This was the afternoon in which his career truly blossomed.

At only one other Australian venue, Adelaide, was he to be even more potent a match-winner.

In all, Warne was chiefly responsible for the winning of 25

Left: Adelaide, 1989: With the Don and Greg Blewett at the Australian Cricket Academy

of his 144 Tests at a rate of one every five or six Tests, a formidable strike-rate ensuring his status in any elite XI from any era.

Even Don Bradman couldn't claim to have been as important as often, but then again the Don played only 52 Tests and was robbed of some of his finest years by World War Two.

Analysing his impact on matches, it's little wonder why he is held in such exulted status as he was directly responsible for 12 Australian wins in his 52 Tests, at a rate of one every four or five Tests; a slightly superior strike-rate to Warne.

In the last 47 of his 52 Tests, the Don never scored a century for a losing side. Ten of his tons came in matches Australia won by an innings. The most important of those were probably 232 at the Oval in 1930 and 234 at Sydney in 1946-47.

TESTS WARNIE 'WON'

	Analysis
1. Colombo, 1992	0-107 & 3-11
2. Melbourne, 1992-93	1-65 & 7-52
3. Manchester, 1993	4-51 & 4-86
4. Birmingham, 1993	1-63 & 5-82
5. Brisbane, 1994-95	3-39 & 8-71
6. Melbourne, 1994-95	6-64 & 3-16
7. Brisbane, 1995-96	7-23 & 4-54
8. Sydney, 1996-97	3-65 & 4-95
9. Manchester, 1997	6-48 &3-63
10. Sydney, 1997-98	5-75 & 6-34
11. Wellington, 1999-00	4-65 & 3-92
12. Nottingham, 2001	2-37 & 6-33
13. The Oval, 2001	7-165 & 4-64
14. Adelaide, 2001-02	5-113 & 3-57
15. Cape Town, 2001-02	2-70 & 6-161
16. Colombo, 2002-03	7-94 & 4-94
17. Sharjah, 2002-03	5-74 & 3-56
18. Adelaide, 2002-03	4-93 & 3-36
19. Galle, 2003-04	5-116 & 5-43
20. Kandy, 2003-04	5-65 & 5-90
21. Brisbane, 2004-05	4-97 & 4-15
22. Adelaide, 2005-06	1-77 & 6-80
23. Durban, 2005-06	2-80 & 6-86
24. Adelaide, 2006-07	1-167 & 4-49
25. Melbourne, 2006-07	5-39 & 2-46

TESTS THE DON 'WON'

	Scores
1. Melbourne, 1928-29	123 & 37*
2. Lord's, 1930	254 & 1
3. Melbourne, 1931-32	2 & 167
4. Adelaide, 1931-32	299*
5. Melbourne, 1932-33	0 & 103*
6. The Oval, 1934	244 & 77
7. Melbourne, 1936-37	13 & 270
8. Adelaide, 1936-37	26 & 212
9. Leeds, 1938	103 & 16
10. Melbourne, 1947-48	132 & 127*
11. Nottingham, 1948	138 & 0
12. Leeds, 1948	33 & 173*

* Denotes not out

Statistician Charles Davis says Adelaide, 1947-48, could also be added to the list as he made 201, the only double century in a high-scoring match in which Australia made 674 batting first and India replied with 381 and 277.

Five of the Don's pivotal contributions occurred at the MCG and none in his original home city, Sydney. The Don won nine of his 12 Tests before turning 30, Warnie 15 of his 25 after turning 30.

Brisbane was Warne's most-prolific ground statistically. He was central in three Australian wins there, as he was in Melbourne. But he won four in Adelaide, including the seemingly impossible-to-win second Ashes of 2006-07 after England had declared its first innings closed at 6-551.

Neil Harvey, Australia's finest batsman of the '50s said Bradman was still an extraordinary player after the War. "It must have been truly amazing beforehand," he said.

Warne survived operations to his shoulder and finger and became an even finer bowler late in his career than he'd been when he was at his athletic best in his mid-20s. He breathed fresh life into a dying art.

Former Australian Rodney Hogg says Warne "has to be up there with Bradman as our best ever".

"He is the best bowler of all time. His influence on cricket has been unbelievable," he said.

Right: Old Trafford, 1993: Mike Gatting b Warne 4. Photo: Patrick Eagar

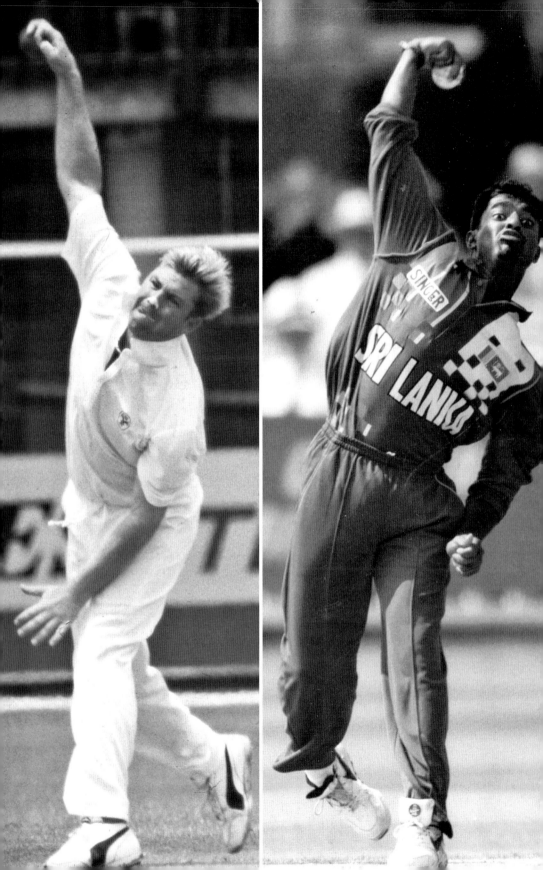

Warne v Murali

***Tiny Muthiah Muralidaran,
the son of a Kandy biscuit maker, is the only one to
surpass Warne's wicket-taking ways***

*L*et Muthiah Muralidaran be the judge: asked where he felt he stood when compared with Shane Warne, he smiled and said: "Warnie... Warnie is the best. Leg spin bowling is so much tougher to do, just from your shoulder rotation. I know I have tried it. It's hard work ... very hard work."

The Sri Lankan genius was having an enforced rest in Melbourne, hoping to avoid a shoulder operation after a decade of bowling more balls in international cricket than anyone, Warne included.

It was 2002 and he was under no illusions to his standing in the world game and not sure just how longer he could continue. We met every morning for a week, taping interviews and talking cricket. His admiration for Warne's big-spinning ways was profound and genuine.

> **"...Warne was the first to the 500 mark but Murali has never been too far behind."**

Milestones that both have now achieved like 700 Test wickets seemed an eternity away, yet both have now forged ahead of some of the best ever including Dennis Lillee, Ian Botham, Richard Hadlee, Wasim Akram and Courtney Walsh.

Warne was the first to the 500 mark but Murali has never been too far behind and with his mysterious doosra, the other one which spins towards slip, he became an even more potent bowler than Warne, especially on home surfaces.

Their illustrious international careers started within months of each other. Both had been fast-tracked, Warne after barely a handful of Sheffield Shield games and Murali virtually straight from school.

Head-to-head comparisons are complicated by the fact that the two played in a very different mix of locations and against different varieties of opponents. Murali has played a much higher proportion of his Tests on home wickets and tends to be more potent at home than away, while Warne has superior overall figures away from Australia.

By most core statistical measures, Murali has been more outstanding and spectacular. He surpasses Warne and by a decisive margin on both bowling average and wickets per match. Murali has, of course, many more five-wicket and 10-wicket hauls, partly due to the fact that he has fewer top-class colleagues to share the wickets with. The two bowlers are neck-and-neck on three-wicket innings hauls, but Murali has a huge lead in five-wicket hauls (60 to 37).

One useful alternative comparison is to analyse their performances under "neutral", but competitive conditions – and by excluding all Tests in Sri Lanka or Australia and also ignoring "Tests" involving Zimbabwe, Bangladesh and the World XI. Curiously, Murali has played only 37 Tests in this higher-level category (from 113), while Warne played 64. But Murali still has the edge: 23.7 to 25.4 on bowling average, and 5.9 to 5.1 on wickets per match.

In the four Test series in which they opposed each other, Warne was superior only once:

1992-93	Warne 3 wickets	Murali 4
1995-96	Warne 12	Murali 3
1999-2000	Warne 8	Murali 15
2003-04	Warne 26	Murali 28

They both played in the ICC-approved exhibition Test in Sydney in 2005-06, Warne taking six wickets and Murali five.

Many will point to the purity of Warne's action compared with the jerkiness of Murali, born with a permanent kink in his elbow. His brother Sasi Daran has the same condition.

In time, it's to be hoped that cricket fans will recognise Murali's freakish talent, just as they have embraced Warne and all his magnificent achievements since his hesitant start in Test cricket from the New Year Test match of 1992.

> *"The best spinner I have ever faced is Shane Warne and is action is 100 per cent legal. So when his stats are compared with Murali's in 20 or 30 years time, the Sri Lankan will almost certainly have the better figures and that will do Shane a disservice because it is he who should really be the leading wicket-taker in Test history. Yes Murali is good for cricket, but is he a better bowler than Shane Warne? I don't think so."*
>
> NASSER HUSSAIN

Tests Played for Milestones

Wicket No.	100	200	300	400	500	600	700
Shane Warne	23	42	63	92	108	126	144
Muthiah Muralidaran	27	42	58	72	87	101	

Lucky breaks

He'd bowl bouncers and even an occasional beamer. He called it his Derryn Hinch ball. Expect the unexpected

*B*rigitte Warne believes her son's ability to make the ball spin and leap has much to do with him having both his legs broken, aged eight, in a schoolyard accident.

His favoured way of getting around was chest down on a pillow on a small, flattened billycart. Mrs Warne said the daily work-outs for the best part of a year helped Shane develop extraordinary strength in his wrists, back and shoulders.

From the age of 11 and 12 when he first began toying with leg-spin in the old nets at East Sandringham, Warne was able to rip the ball like an adult. They didn't always land mind you, but when they did, they jumped and darted sideways like a kid stung by a bumblebee. He enjoyed making batsmen look silly.

He'd alternate between tossing his leggies high into the air and running in fast, trying to bowl like the wind. He imagined he was Dennis Lillee and there were 60,000 at the Melbourne Cricket Ground all calling his name. WARRNNIE... WARRNNIE... WARRNNIE...

Even then the theatre of the centre stage had an irresistible appeal.

Mentors advised him to stick with his wrist spin but despite his promise, he made none of the elite under-age XIs. He was keener on football and on training nights would wear his favourite No.23 Hawthorn guernsey with the long sleeves pushed up *a la* his hero Dermott Brereton. When lining up for goal, he even twiddled the ball in his hands, exactly like Dermott. In one school game, in Launceston he kicked 15 goals and followed with seven in another.

Trevor Barker was another of his idols and when he played a season with St Kilda's third XVIII in 1988, many at Moorabbin called him "Young Barks". One of his teammates in the Under 19s was 16-year-old Robert Harvey who became one of the legends of the AFL.

Despite winning promotion to the reserves, he wasn't considered fast enough for his size, and much to his disappointment he was delisted. Thanks ... but no thanks.

A few of his mates from St Kilda CC had headed to England during the off-season and he and 19-year-old Ricky Gough opted to go, too, to Bristol for the 1989 northern summer.

They mixed their cricket with non-stop partying.

They were gloriously uninhibited days with an extended send-off which seemed to go forever. A video of the shenanigans was made, Gough wisely retrieving it before they left. The tabloids would have loved it ...

It was the first time Warne had ever lived away from home and he stacked on so much weight on a diet of chip rolls and numerous pints that his father Keith barely recognised him when he picked him up from Tullamarine.

His captain at St Kilda, Shaun Graf, was also astonished at the transformation. He immediately made him run the Albert Park Lake, twice, before dropping him to the thirds.

So peeved was Warne that he almost gave up then and there

and seriously contemplated a return to park cricket. He felt he'd done enough with the St Kilda second XI late the previous season to warrant consideration for a promotion to the firsts – not a demotion to the thirds.

Having shed at least some of the unwanted pounds, Warne was soon elevated to the first XI, his sheer skill outweighing any differences of opinion over his still expansive waistline.

Before one of his earliest matches Graf and Victorian club legend John Scholes were exchanging team sheets and Scholes read down the St Kilda list. All the names were familiar, except for Warne's. Looking around, he pointed at Warne with his peroxided hair, earring and only just fitting into his top and said: "Who's Hulk Hogan?"

> *"He was huge, like a beached whale. He had all this blond hair and was simply very, very fat. I thought, 'Who the hell is this bloke'?"*
> Warne's St Kilda teammate LAURIE HARPER

*W*arnie was carting beds for a living for Forty Winks back then. Tuesdays and Thursdays were always days of particular focus so his cricket training time would not be affected.

Invariably he'd be the first to arrive and he'd do flat-out circuits of the old Junction Oval in his hotted-up cream Cortina, always with the stereo at full tilt.

Warnie and those big mag wheels survived a few scrapes along the way. One night just near Darby's in Caulfield he spun out, doing a 360 in wet weather. Car and Warnie emerged unscathed.

The 21st Century night club was another favourite haunt, his

affability invariably an all-round winner.

He played hard on and off the field, but what really impressed his cricketing mates at St Kilda was his insatiable work ethic in the nets. He built on the momentum he'd created in England, bowling for hours on end. It was noticeable, too, how often he was beating even the experienced players.

"He'd improved dramatically in just six months," said St Kilda's former Sheffield Shield opener David Robinson. "All of a sudden you couldn't hit him. He had the flight right, the trajectory, and the line and length. He was really zipping them around."

Back then and even when first chosen for Australia, the emerging leggie didn't have any particular plan or strategy. He simply tried to spin the cover off the ball.

Having played his first Test match in Sydney and gone for 150 runs for just one wicket, his mates asked him why he hadn't used his googly.

Always honest, he said: "I was afraid it would bounce twice."

*W*arne's head-turning ability to fizz the ball, combined with his ready smile and intuition to rapidly learn new tricks of the trade were integral in his fast-tracking. He had a cricket brain and was a natural leader. He was also charismatic and fun to be around.

So impressed was Victorian state coach Ian Redpath when he saw him by chance in the nets that soon Warne was heading to Adelaide as part of the new intake to the Australian Cricket Academy. Spinners were in short supply in Australia. The West Indian formula of four fast bowlers was being mimicked around the world. And why not! They'd been world champions for years.

At the Academy, head coach Jack Potter spoke with Warne about his variations and in particular an lbw ball. Years earlier Potter had toured with Australian teams as a specialist batsman, but he'd also experimented with leggies and knew how to bowl a flipper, the quicker skidding ball which Richie Benaud had used so successfully.

They went to the Adelaide indoor nets and stood end to end bowling the ball back and forth.

Potter had been told that the kid could spin it. But he had no idea how much. He really ripped them.

Every now and again Potter would amble down the wicket and make a subtle suggestion or two. He noted that Warne "telegraphed" his googly, but it still spun. Sharply.

After 10 minutes or so, Potter said: "That's enough for now, Shane", and the two chatted expansively, Potter saying how much he liked Warne's leg-break. It bounced. It spun. It dipped.

"But Shane," said Potter, "it's also predictable. Do you know what? The best players are going to wait for the bad one and simply pick you off. You need to have something else ... an lbw ball. Something which is flatter, straighter, quicker."

He talked about the Benaud flipper and how it had doubled his effectiveness, Warne listening with growing fascination. He'd missed all the elite junior squads as a teenager and even then was probably keener on becoming a football star, but Potter was unveiling exciting new mysteries, things he'd never even considered before.

The pair had several sessions in the following weeks, Warne determined to master the new delivery. His early attempts had seen one delivery sail head-high past Potter. Another was so wide it would have decapitated the bloke at bat-pad.

Two of Warne's greatest strengths, however, have always been his work ethic and his ability to absorb lessons. Within a fortnight, he had the new delivery down pat. It spat out the front of his hand, much like a pip from an orange before hurrying straight and flat at the off stump. Potter's digs were in Port Adelaide and down the corridor one night, Warnie said –"watch this" and bowled two or three perfect flippers. He'd got it.

In the months ahead, working with another former Australian, Terry Jenner, Warne was to refine and develop the delivery and truly understand its mechanics. But Potter remains firmly in his debt, having introduced a challenging fresh dimension to his game which Warne instinctively knew was going to be important.

Within years, Warne was to become known as the flipperman, the affable kid from Melbourne's seaside suburbs who mixed a leg-break from heaven with a delicious faster one.

A Young Australian side was due to tour the West Indies and Warne was chosen, the only one from outside the national Under 19 squad.

Even Warne's fellow Victorians like Damien Fleming had never met him before. He was a bolter, an absolute unknown.

By the tour's end he'd been voted the most popular Australian player. His bleached snowy white hair had also prompted a range of fresh nicknames from "Billy" (after rock icon Billy Idol) to "The White Knight". His mates liked the way he did everything at 100 mph, whether it was poolside dancing at Montego Bay, straddling a cannon at jockey Scobie Breasley's Caribbean paradise or lying

down on the baggage conveyor belts and pretending he was asleep at Barbados airport. Each of the tourists was given a video for posterity. It's a scream.

Team manager Brian Taber, the former Australian wicketkeeper, had been instructed if any player stepped over the line, behaviour-wise, that they be sent straight home. But there wasn't a hint of trouble from anyone. "Warnie was probably the best tourist of the lot," he said.

Soon after his return, Warne met Jenner at the nets at the Adelaide Oval.

Jenner had been the wrist spinner in Ian Chappell's champion Australian teams of the early '70s and was dabbling with cricket coaching. Potter had helped set up the meeting. "There's someone I'd like you to meet Shane," he said. "He could be very helpful to you."

They shook hands and there was an immediate empathy. Marching out to the nets at Adelaide Oval No.2, Jenner said: "Show me what you've got, Shane."

The first one dipped and spun sharply and ripped into Jenner's bare hands, leaving a clear imprint. "Jeesus Fuckkinn' Christ," he said.

"Try another one Shane."

The second one spun even further.

Jenner shook his head and smiled. This kid was special.

*B*efore Warne's emergence, leggies tended to bowl like millionaires, generally conceding at least one "four ball" per over. They were tolerated in four-day games, but shunned at one-day level. Captains tended to use only those who could contain and run through their overs quickly.

Warne was to re-write the rules, his phenomenal accuracy allowing captains to immediately surround a batsman with close-in catchers. When Warne was introduced, it was game on, from ball one, like at Old Trafford in '93 when England's No.3 Mike Gatting was famously castled first-up by a monster leg-break merely intended to be a warm-up ball.

On the tour of New Zealand in '93, leading into his celebrated Ashes beginning, Warne told me he'd bowled only six bad balls all tour. I checked the overall tour stats and he sent down 1127 deliveries at an average of almost 50 overs per match. That's one, maybe two, poor balls per game! No wonder he bowled Gatt!

On this day Gatting had played defensively. Forward, nose over the ball, everything behind it. Warne loved it when batsmen defended but he loved it even more when they looked to set the agenda and play shots. He always felt it gave him more of a chance of sending them packing.

In time he was to develop such an intuitive eye that he could predict a batsman's intentions just by his body language.

The West Indian Carl Hooper was giving the Australians and particularly Warne a hard time during a set of one-day games in the Caribbean. He'd either charge just as Warne was about to release or play dead-bat defence. It was a curious mixture and it was hard to combat too, until Warne studied a video of Hooper, looking for clues.

He particularly watched Hooper in his stance, preparing to face up. "Got it!" he said within minutes. When Hooper intended to stay in his crease, he'd look down at his feet before looking up again just as Warne was beginning his approach. But if he was ready to leave his crease and attack, he'd stare intently down the wicket back at Warne, just waiting to spring.

Hooper was never as menacing against the Australians again. Warne had such a command of his craft he was able to vary his lengths at an inkling.

Warne worked, too, on the minds of opposing batsmen,

Pakistan's Basit Ali falling at Sydney to the last ball of the day (in 1995-96) after deliberately stalling Warne in his approach.

Not wanting another over to be bowled, he took an eternity to settle in his crease and when he was finally ready, Warne paused in his run-up, told umpire Dickie Bird he was going around the wicket and walked down the wicket to talk to captain Mark Taylor and one or two others. Nothing much was said, except for: "It's been a good day, hasn't it!"

Warnie moved a fieldsman half a step one way and another half a step the other and eye-balled Basit, just letting him know who was in control.

A leg break pitched wide outside the leg stump spun between Basit's legs and hit the top of his middle stump. Bird called it "an unbelievable delivery".

"Warne could be excused for his unrestrained war dance of delight," he later wrote.

Like Ian Botham before him, Warne made a habit of changing the momentum of matches.

He'd bowl bouncers and even an occasional beamer. He called it his Derryn Hinch ball. Expect the unexpected.

Shane by Shane II

DREAMS "Basically I wanted to be a footy player. It wasn't until I was 13 or 14 that I started playing junior cricket and was shown the basics of leg-spin. I've no idea why I stuck with it. I could never land the bloody thing!"

JIG-A-JIGGING IN THE UK "The team's great performance, the relief I felt at winning the series and the effects of all the abuse I'd copped throughout the tour got to me and I went too far. I reacted emotionally and went over the top a bit." (1993)

HIS BRAIN SNAP "I got a bit cocky and a bit arrogant. I did a couple of things in South Africa I am ashamed of when I sledged Andrew Hudson. I just couldn't believe I did that." (1993-94)

WORKING BOY "I think nothing of bowling 30 or 40 overs, but ask me to run eight kilometres and I struggle."

SUB-CONTINENT BOUND "I'm not a great fan of Indian food and I've packed three jumbo-size jars of Vegemite to keep me going."

ON TERRY JENNER "When T.J. said something I listened, which was not always the case with the coaches at the Academy."

DUMPED IN THE WINDIES "I have to have a serious think about what I want to do in the future." (1999)

PERCEPTIONS "A certain percentage of the public out there just don't like you for whatever reason; they're jealous of you, they just don't like the way you conduct yourself or the way you play – they think you're arrogant. All you can do is be yourself."

21st Century Girl,
Simone & Other Stories

Fun-loving, cocksure and charismatic. That's our Warnie...

*E*veryone has a story about Shane Warne, even my local gardener.

Warnie was still in his teens and a very pretty girl was umm... err... keen – exceptionally keen – to get up close and personal.

They were at the 21st Century Dance Club in Frankston and she and her mates would always be hanging out for Warnie and his.

Years later one of the blokes recognised her on television: "That's the girl from the 21st who had the enormous crush on Warnie".

She'd been one of the featured guests in Princess Mary's wedding party.

*B*aked beans and tinned spaghetti ... it has long been a staple of Warnie's, but he admits too much of either isn't a desirable social habit.

During one Indian tour, he'd asked for a few tins to be sent over as an occasional "delicacy".

Rather than few tins, SPC, now a key sponsor, sent over several crate loads, almost all of which was given to charity.

Left: Melbourne, 1993-94

Warnie first met Simone Callahan, his soulmate and mother of his three kids, at a charity golf day at Royal Melbourne Golf Club. He was playing and she was one of the very leggy Foster's promotions girls handing out freebies.

"She gave me her phone number," said Warne, "and I said to myself: 'Whatever happens don't lose this'!"

"I put the piece of paper in with a packet of cigarettes but the next morning I couldn't find it. I must have finished my packet of fags and thrown them and the number away!

"I wasn't impressed as I didn't know where she worked or how to get in contact with her. It all faded out and then I saw her again at the Saloon bar (in Toorak Road, South Yarra) five or six months later (the night he made a Victorian-best 69 against Western Australia).

"She was playing pool with a friend and they were winning. They wouldn't get off the table. I was trying to say hello and I asked for her phone number again and she said: 'No way!'

(While Warnie was explaining all this, his then girlfriend Simone was in the same room laughing).

"I said: 'Well, here's my phone number, please give me a ring,' but she never did.

A month later at another charity day, they met again. "We called it a truce. I rang and we got together."

They were to be engaged in 1993 and married in 1995, having three kids: daughters Brooke and Summer and a son, Jackson.

In 2005, after having publicly announced several times that Warne was on his "last chance", Simone grew sick of the continuing headlines prompted by her husband's night-time activities and returned to Melbourne with their children. They divorced in 2006.

A nervous young Warnie was at the Adelaide Oval nets for the first time bowling to the legendary David Hookes. The first ball was on leg stump and as it spun away, "Hookesy" took a hand off his bat and one-handed it back to Warne with a contemptuous: "Don't bowl there son."

B rian McMillan was one of the more charismatic South African cricketers of the '90s, chatty and provocative with rare perspective. He was a sportsman being paid to play the game he loved, and while seriously competitive, he loved to have a bit of fun on the side.

McMillan was big on gamesmanship and like Warnie, used it as a genuine weapon to unsettle his opponents.

From his position in gully, Warnie thought McMillan's ample hooter matched that of the prominent French actor Gerard Depardieu (*Green Card* etc) so to the amusement of the Australian slip fielders he started calling him "Depardieu".

"C'mon boys, let's get Depardieu out," he said.

Warne maintained the banter and soon afterwards chided McMillan for not running a three, saying: "Looks like you don't fancy it (the strike) very much Depardieu."

"Listen Warnie," said McMillan, "You're coming to South Africa soon. People disappear every day over there. One more won't make any difference!"

He threatened to take Warnie fishing – and feed him to the sharks!

Another time, in Johannesburg, after an on-field grilling, McMillan entered the Australians' rooms at a break, armed with an AK47 pistol he'd borrowed from a nearby security officer: "Right

you Australians," he said, shaping to shoot them all. "I've had enough of you."

Everyone hit the deck, not daring to look.

McMillan 1, Australia 1.

$\mathcal{H}$aving dobbed fellow leg-spinner and friend Mushtaq Ahmed for several sixes on his way to a whirlwind 86 in a 'Gabba Test (Brisbane, 1999), Warnie was seeing just how many rows back the latest one had flown when confronted in mid-pitch by little Mushie, red-faced and indignant: "What are you doing?" he said. "What am I doing wrong with you?"

"Sorry Mushie," said Warnie. "I don't fancy Waqar (Younis, Pakistan's express bowler), so it's your time. Wherever you bowl I'm just going to close my eyes and slog!"

$\mathcal{W}$arnie's bunny Daryll Cullinan had just taken guard when a voice from short leg said: "I'm here to help you!"

He didn't even glance around, let alone say anything.

"The first ball will be a small leg-break," said the voice, "so soft hands and just play it away."

It was and he did.

"Do you trust me now?" said the voice.

Cullinan smiled.

"Next will be a big leggie and Warnie often drags it down so you should cut it for four through the gap at point and get off the mark!"

It was the big leggie and he let it go.

"Idiot!" said the voice. "But... do you trust me now!"

He smiled again.

"Next will be the top spinner so come forward with nice soft hands and you will be fine."

He did.

"Do you trust me now?"

Cullinan almost laughed this time.

"Okay Daryll," said the voice. "Here comes the flipper. Now for God's sake, no matter what you see out of the hand, GO FORWARD!"

He went back, lbw Warne 0.

David Boon still reckons he should have trusted him.

*P*at Symcox was a feisty, mature-age offie who was also good enough, once, to score a Test century.

In Sydney, the match in which South Africa broke through for an amazing come-from-behind victory (1993-94), Warnie bowled him around his legs for seven, immediately after he'd padded the preceding ball away and yelled down the wicket: "You'll never get me there, boy!"

*S*teve Waugh and Warnie loved to hate Nasser Hussain, the ever-so-intense England No.4. "C'mon let's get dodgy technique out" or "Let's get Mr Popular out," Warnie would yell.

Australia's 12th man Justin Langer had come on as a sub-fieldsman at Edgbaston (1997) and immediately joined in, too.

"Look," Hussain hissed between overs, "I don't mind this lot (Warne, Waugh and Co.) chirping me, but you've just come on. You're the fucking bus driver in this team."

$\mathcal{H}$aving taken two wickets in two balls, Warnie was on a hat-trick in a Test match in front of his own home crowd (1994-95). Eyeing who was coming in next, non-striker Alec Stewart said to Warne: "You'll never get a better chance than this!"

Just as everyone was re-taking their positions, Damien Fleming walked past Warne and joked, "Listen mate, do you really want to know how to get your hat-trick?"

"Yeah, how?"

"Well, I'd close my eyes and try to think of bowling the perfect yorker or the big outswinger … my wicket-taking balls," said 'Flemo'. "When I was going for my hat-trick [at Rawalpindi, just months earlier], I was thinking about bowling a bouncer, a slower ball or a yorker.

I thought I'd stick with my stock delivery [the outswinger], because that is the ball which comes through for me eight times out of 10."

Warne nodded, deep in thought, before producing an over-spinning leg-break, which bounced and spun, caught Devon Malcolm on the gloves and splayed to the right of short leg David Boon, who took a finger-tipper diving to his right. A delighted Warne charged across the wicket and picked "Boonie" up in a bear hug. It was the first hat-trick of his life, even including the juniors at East Sandringham.

"It came out just as I wanted," he told us all at the press

conference at the old VCA delegate's room afterwards. "I just got lucky."

The scorebook entry for his memorable 13th over read: 3. . XXX.

Questions Without Notice

QUESTION: Why do you call him (Salim Malik) the Rat?"
WARNIE: "Because he looks like one."

QUESTION from the English team to tail-ender Devon Malcolm who presented Shane Warne with a Test hat-trick: "Why didn't you have a go at him, Dev?"
MALCOLM: "I was going to, but then I thought I'd try and play properly!"

*I*t was a bouncy one in Trinidad (1995) and batting was a genuine health hazard. Warnie was in with Paul Reiffel, both intent on trying to keep at the non-striker's end for as long as possible.

"Basically we were shitting ourselves," said Reiffel. "It was tough out there."

Courtney Walsh was charging in and when Warnie got a nick, the look of relief on his face was enormous. He was beginning to walk off when the umpire said: "No, not out."

"Oh no," said an anguished Warnie, hardly believing the umpire could get it so wrong,

13 Batsmen Warnie Dismissed Most In Tests

Times

14	Alec Stewart (England)
11	Nasser Hussain (England), Ashwell Prince (South Africa)
10	Mike Atherton (England)
9	Graham Thorpe (England), Steve Harmison (England)
8	Andy Caddick (England), Hansie Cronje (South Africa), Ashley Giles (England), Craig McMillan (New Zealand), Dave Richardson (South Africa), Marcus Trescothick (England)
4	Daryll Cullinan (South Africa)

No-one that day wanted to get in behind Courtney, Curtly Ambrose and Co!

The wicket was soft and totally unsuitable for Test cricket, the Australians lasting only 47 overs in the first innings and less than 40 in the second.

*E*nglishman Robert Croft was admiring his handiwork having lifted Warnie for six in the final stanzas of a one-day at Trent Bridge (1997). He delayed facing up again so he could catch a glimpse of himself on the instant replay screen.

"Hey Crofty," said Warne, "You'll be able to see the replay again in a couple of minutes." (When you're out.)

Sure enough, within an over or two, Croft was out, for six, caught by "Pigeon" McGrath bowled Warne.

*W*arnie hadn't played for a month (in 1997) and ran headlong into the in-form South African hitter Adrian Kuiper who helped himself to two sixes from Warnie's bowling and three overall in a one-dayer in Sydney. Later, Warne said he was so rusty he'd forgotten his run-up.

That was the summer Hansie Cronje hit one of the biggest sixes from Warne's bowling in Sydney onto the roof of the Bill O'Reilly Stand.

The New Zealander Chris Cairns consistently hit Warnie further than anyone else, though. One mighty smite Warne claimed could only come back "with Frequent Flyer" points on it!

*E*xchanging shirts with Daryll Cullinan after the epic World Cup tie at Edgbaston (1999), Warnie couldn't help but laugh when Cullinan quipped: "I expect this will go in the bunnies' section!"

At The Oval (2001), the Australian team burnt a ball to create their own Ashes, only to set off the smoke alarms!

> *"Tick, tock, tick, tock, tick, tock, tick, tock, tick, tock." – WARNIE and Victoria's wicketkeeper Darren Berry to a struggling Michael Slater during a Sheffield Shield match.*
> *"I know what they were getting at,"* Slater said later. *"They reckoned I was a time bomb waiting to explode."*

*I*mpulsive? Promiscuous? Foolhardy? Or is Warnie a target? Misunderstood? Unlucky?

Shane Warne says he has made choices and because of his celebrity, so have many women who have kissed-and-told of their flings with him, triggering fresh circulation spirals for the London tabloids.

The text and voice messages have been a constant, many of the one-night and two-night stand women saying he had "bombarded" them with racy messages.

Unauthorised biographer Paul Barry said Warne's marriage had been a sham from early days, Warne's roving eye and his attraction to women providing a lethal combination. He cited a fleet of women linked to Warne from old girlfriends on his first trips to the UK to those paid by newspapers to get him to bed and tell their stories.

Warne and wife Simone divorced in 2006, the final straw in a reconciliation coming in mid-year 2007 via yet another Warnie text message gone wrong:

HEY BEAUTIFUL. I'M JUST TALKING TO MY KIDS. THE BACK DOOR IS OPEN.

It had been sent to her, by mistake, she alleged. She was back in Melbourne and he was in the UK.

YOU LOSER

she texted back,

YOU SENT THE MESSAGE TO THE WRONG PERSON.

In a paid interview with *New Idea*, she said she had been suspicious for some time that Warne "was up to his old tricks".

"Deep down in my heart I knew sooner or later that he'd do it again ... a leopard doesn't change its spots."

Warne also released a statement saying that the pair had been divorced for more than a year and had separated once and for all in August 2007. He was photographed hurrying with his luggage into Heathrow, for once not enjoying his notoriety.

Newspapers ran polls asking was Simone better off without Shane. More than 80 per cent said "yes".

VOTELINE

Yesterday's result

Is Simone better off without Shane Warne?

82.9%

17.1%

1300
1040
780
520
260

1242
YES

256
NO

TOTAL 1498 VOTES

ADAMANT: Readers of the Melbourne *Herald-Sun* were adamant, when polled, that Simone was better off without Shane after his latest phone escapades in England in the 2007 northern summer.

YOU KNOW. NO ONE EVER TAKES A POLL ABOUT WHETHER I'M BETTER OFF WITHOUT SIMONE!

"Shane Warne is God's gift to cricket,"
SACHIN TENDULKAR

"Shane Warne was a nobody, so far as the majority of Englishmen were concerned. A boy off the beaches, bleached and bronzed as if auditioning for *Neighbours*."
Prominent English cricket writer and author ALAN LEE

"He's the sort of guy who, if we keep him fresh, will be a match-winner for us for many years to come. He's only 25. We have to make sure the warning signs don't get too bad and force him out of the game before we can do something about it."
Australian captain MARK TAYLOR (1994)

"Make no mistake (Stuart) MacGill was a real threat. He turned the ball more than Warne and his googly was much trickier, but he was still only about three-quarters the bowler Warne was, as much in character as anything else. MacGill had only a fraction of Warne's character and that's why Australia was much the poorer for Shane Warne's absence."
England's NASSER HUSSAIN speaking of Warne's absence for most of the 1998-99 Ashes campaign

"A little known blond-haired kid with a mullet, who looked like the love child of new PGA golf champion John Daly blew everyone on tour away with his freakish ability and enthusiasm for a battle."
STEVE WAUGH on Warne's first senior tour overseas, to Zimbabwe

"Two things made him exceptional: his control and the amount of action he gets on the ball, giving him more drift in the air than any other spinner I have played against."
Former England captain MIKE ATHERTON

"He [Warne] is the only guy I've watched since I retired to cause the hair to stand up on the back of my neck."
Australian pace bowling great DENNIS LILLEE

"Warne had endured his share of controversy, but no-one would question his place in any hall of fame and he was rated as one of the five cricketers of the 20th century by *Wisden*."
ABC commentator JIM MAXWELL

"No bowler has ever arrived in the Caribbean with greater advance billing than the bouncy, blond leg-spinner. His encounter with the superstar batsman of the moment, Lara, was the stuff of which cricket lovers' dreams are made."
West Indian writer and commentator TONY COZIER (1995)

"For me Warne is in the J. P. McEnroe class; he is so good to watch that I'll watch him no matter how badly he performs."
Author JACK EGAN

"We might have been mates for a few years, but the bat-ball contest is always very competitive. He wants me to attack him, come down the wicket and hit him for four or six. I'd like to oblige but Warnie keeps getting me out!"
DARREN GOUGH (1997)

"Shane was at his peak from the ages of 24 to 26. Since then, he's had to adapt his thinking to a new set of standards and a new feeling when bowling his leg-break. He has to work a lot harder for his wickets now. If he was the same bowler from the point of view of whip and grip, you just can't consistently play that standard of bowling."

Warne's coach, TERRY JENNER

"How a man can continue to do what he does on a diet of pizza and cigarettes will continue to confound the sports fitness experts."

JONATHON RICE

"It was an amazing ball. Long after we've all retired, that one delivery will be etched in the memory of everyone who witnessed it."

STEVE WAUGH on *that ball* (1993)

"He is an enormously proud person and loves to show you his new toys, just like a little kid on Christmas Day. It doesn't matter if it's a new car, laptop computer, clothing, music system or house."

DARREN BERRY

"Warnie has been the biggest influence on cricket in my time. Spin bowling was dying until he burst onto the scene. Look around now: spin bowlers everywhere. That's down to Warnie. Not just his ability but his looks, his personality – the whole package. He has given cricket a new dimension."

DARREN GOUGH

"If you want to know how the respective merits of Warne and Benaud compare in regard to bowling, you need look no further than one statistic. When Warne reached his 300th Test wicket he was playing in his 63rd Test, the same number I played in my whole career to take 248. Statistics sometimes lie but definitely not this one: he is that much better than I was. I had batting and fielding and captaincy to help me in any all-round ratings but Warne is the best of his kind I've ever seen."

RICHIE BENAUD

"He is the best I have seen of any kind and undoubtedly the best bowler Australia has produced since Bill O'Reilly."

Ex-Test opener COLIN McDONALD

"He loves a cigarette, a quiet drink, his children, his football club, in this case St Kilda, and the camaraderie of a cricket team. He's also a generous man towards his close friends."

Melbourne journalist JON PIERIK

"Star status is also evident by the way the public whisper when they are near him, as though he were a Hollywood actor. From undermining young batsmen (and those who should know better) to charming catering staff into making an extra cheese sandwich, he carries extraordinary force of personality."

English journalist RICHARD HOBSON

"I may be getting soft after all the celebrations, but I don't believe Warne ever deserved to be on the losing side."

ANDREW FLINTOFF (2006)

Eleven Of The Best

Shane Warne's 11 best ever wickets from **that ball** *at Old Trafford, the most-acclaimed ever ...*

1 **Mike Gatting (England) b.Warne 4, Old Trafford, 1993**

With his first ball in an Ashes Test, Warne produced the jaffa of his career which curved and spun wickedly across Gatting, beating his defensive prod and clipping his off bail.

Warne ran down the wicket with his fist clenched in triumph. A thunderstruck Gatting was frozen to the crease in shock. Finally he looked at square leg umpire Ken Palmer, received a nod that "yes", he was out, bowled and off he belatedly trudged, shaking his head.

Pandemonium reigned as the Australians celebrated in a tight circle. Merv Hughes was boundary riding square of the wicket and raced in and asked wicketkeeper Ian Healy what had happened. "Heals told me: 'Pitched off, hit off.' We watched a replay and I saw this thing swerve in the air, pitch outside leg and spin almost at right angles before just clipping the top of the off bail. 'It might have done a bit, Heals,' I said."

It was *that ball*, The Ball of the Century, the most celebrated and talked about delivery in Ashes annals.

2 **Richie Richardson (WI) b. Warne 52, Melbourne, 1992-93**

Until that memorable Melbourne Christmas, Warne's international career was lurching, his famed self-belief waning.

Walking with Ian Healy down through Yarra Park into the MCC members, he confessed his confidence was shot. He was thinking of how embarrassing it would be to be hit all over the park again, in his home town, in front of all his mates.

A Healy pep-talk and a spot-on flipper which castled the West Indian captain Richardson changed everything.

Not only did it swing a Test match in Boys' Own Annual fashion, giving Australia its solitary win of the summer, it was the makings of one of the great careers of all. No leg-spinner since the days of legendary Bill O'Reilly had ever been as successful in a Melbourne Test. "I'll wake up soon," a disbelieving Warne told us all in the press conference afterwards.

3 Shivnarine Chanderpaul (West Indies) b. Warne 71, Sydney, 1996-97

The Gatting leg-break may be more celebrated and the Richardson flipper more important in terms of the bigger career picture, but this was probably the most spectacular and satisfying of all.

Finger surgery during the off-season had left Warne hesitant and highly protective of his hands, so much so that he even resorted to greeting old friends with his left, rather than his right hand.

Having had little impact in the first Test, despite bowling a mountain of overs, Warne was still far from comfortable in Sydney.

Set 340 to win, the West Indies seemed an outside chance on the final day with tiny Guyanese left-hander Chanderpaul rushing to 71 from just 68 balls. At 3-152 and the Chanderpaul - Carl Hooper partnership blossoming, a West Indian win was still not impossible as Warne began his last over before lunch.

Before his fifth delivery, Warne paused. He told himself he

Team Talk

"Until then [the Sri Lanka tour], Shane knew little about taking wickets, relied on his natural talent and bowled without great expectation. His body language was poor and he seemed to feel he'd done the job when the ball left his hand. I instilled in him the importance of following through aggressively, which gave him even more spin and bounce and put greater pressure on the batsmen."

Warne's first national coach, BOB SIMPSON

"Shane is always prepared to try something and think in the positive. He's always receptive to me trying to winkle batsmen out. That's why I like him. He's prepared to back himself."

Warne's first captain, ALLAN BORDER

"Shane Warne came into the Australian team at just the right time as far as my career was concerned."

IAN HEALY

"He gambles. I don't. I like hot curries. He likes plain food. He's a glamour. I'm not. He's young. I'm not. It goes on and on."

TIM MAY on his mid-'90s spin partnership with Warne

"I like bowling in tandem with Shane. We feed off the other's hard work until something "gives" with the batsman."

GLENN McGRATH

could no longer "nurse" his finger. Bowling from around the wicket, he gave the ball the biggest possible "rip". It pitched almost on the return crease and miraculously darted back from the footmarks and flicked Chanderpaul's pad on the way through to hitting his leg stump. It was an extraordinary ball and the shell-shocked Windies were bowled out by 3.30 pm for just 215. Australia 2-nil.

4 Herschelle Gibbs (South Africa) b. Warne 30, World Cup, Edgbaston, 1999

One of his coach Terry Jenner's all-time favorites and the ball which turned the World Cup and revived Warne's career. Chasing only 214, the South Africans were comfortably placed at 0-48 before Warne captured 3-0 in eight deliveries.

Having made 30 from just 36 balls, Gibbs was beaten by a Gatting-type delivery which pitched outside leg and hit off. Wicketkeeper Adam Gilchrist had the best seat in the house and said it was simply unplayable. A pumped-up Warne's mid-pitch celebration was as emotional as any in his celebrated career, his COME-ONNN echoing around the ground.

In a game rated the greatest one-day match of all time, the Proteas could only force a tie and missed qualifying for the final, which the Australians won comfortably.

5 Andrew Strauss (England), b. Warne 6, Edgbaston, 2005

The heat was rapidly being turned on the world champions by a resurgent England. Having lost in four days at Lord's, the Englishmen had hit back to lead by 99 runs to the joy of a rowdy, partying crowd. Throughout his career Warne had made a habit of taking a key wicket and swinging the momentum Australia's way. He knew he had to make some early inroads if England's lead was to be restricted. Introduced early into the attack, he came from wide on the right hand return crease and conjured a Gatting-type ball which the left-handed Strauss offered no shot at, only to watch in horror as it bit and spun viciously to hit his middle and leg stumps.

It was an amazing delivery and in Warne's own words: "One of the best I've ever bowled". Warne took six for 46 in the finest spell I'd witnessed from him. England was bowled out for 182, setting up the grand-daddy of all finishes.

Sitting at fine leg, 100 metres from the action, our tour group were as stunned as Strauss. It seemed inconceivable that a ball could grip and spin back as much as it did. The replay confirmed the dismissal and even the rowdies in the Eric Hollies Stand had to applaud. It was a stunning delivery.

6 Graham Gooch (England) b. Warne 48, Edgbaston, 1993

This was a wicket concocted in the bar the night before, Warne suggesting to Captain Allan Border that a change of line may affect Gooch's rhythm. He'd been in rare form, being the powerhouse batsman in world cricket in the early 1990s. Going around the wicket, Warne's spitting leg-break spun from wide outside Gooch's pads to hit his leg stump. It was a huge wicket which effectively ended the English fightback, the home team plunging to an eight wicket loss, their fourth in five Tests.

7 Sourav Ganguly (India) stumped Gilchrist, b. Warne 60, Adelaide, 1999-00

Bowling with the second new ball for one of the few times in his career, Warne set Ganguly up with multiple leg breaks before producing a googly which the advancing Indian left-hander read too late. Passing between his bat and pad and onto wicketkeeper Adam Gilchrist, he was stranded in mid-pitch, Warne repeatedly pumping his arm in jubilation.

Earlier Ganguly had several times lofted Warne high over the cover field, adding to Warne's satisfaction. Of all of Warne's 700-plus dismissals, less than 25 came with genuine wrong-'uns. This was a standout. Guess who had turned a match again!

The Australians won the Test comfortably, one of their 16 wins in a row, a new record of invincibility unlikely to be beaten for years.

8 Saeed Anwar (Pakistan) b. Warne 78, Hobart, 1999-00

After Saqlain Mushtaq had triggered an amazing Australian collapse from 1-191 to 246 all out, the first time most of the Australians had ever encountered the "doosra", Pakistan was rapidly working towards a shock ascendancy at Bellerive when Warne beat Saeed Anwar, one of his top 10 opponents, with a quick, flat leggie which Anwar shaped to cut only to see his leg stump flattened.

This was the game in which Justin Langer and Adam Gilchrist both scored hundreds, launching one of Australia's great come-from-behind wins.

9 Kevin Pietersen (England) b. Warne 2, Adelaide, 2006-07

Few Australians wins have ever been as spectacular and once again, Warne claimed the key wicket of England's No.1 player, who had made 158 in the first innings, helping England amass 551 before a declaration.

It seemed the match would finish as a dull draw on the final afternoon until England froze, hardly playing a shot and caving in insipidly. Coming in at No. 5, Pietersen tried to change the pace but played "a nervelessly extravagant shot", according to *Wisden*, to be bowled around his legs, Warne operating over the wicket. It was a huge breakthrough in the context of the game and one of four for Warne in yet another command performance.

10 Salim Malik (Pakistan) c. McDermott b. Warne 0, Brisbane, 1995-96

After the prolonged betting controversy in which Warne, Mark Waugh and Tim May were implicated, relations with Salim Malik were icy, the Australians agreeing not to speak, or even acknowledge him – on or off the field.

His first meeting with the Australians since the controversial '94 tour was at the 'Gabba and after injuring his hand early, he didn't bat until the second innings.

To his fourth ball from Warne, a well-tossed leg-break delivered above the eyes, he went to drive only to spoon it tamely to Craig McDermott at mid-off. It was a soft dismissal from a regulation ball, but it was Manna from heaven for Warne after Malik had tried to bribe Warne and Tim May to bowl poorly during the Karachi Test of '94.

Even before the catch was taken, Warne was punching the air in jubilation. "It goes to show that there is justice in the game," an emotional Warne said afterwards. "I've been pretty down. Mum (Brigitte), Dad (Keith) and my wife (Simone) got me through. I'd like to dedicate the wicket to them especially."

The Australians won by an innings, Warne taking a cool 11 wickets for the match.

11 Alec Stewart (England) b. Warne 33, Brisbane, 1994-95

This was another triumph for the Flipperman and one of eight wickets for the innings, his finest ever Test analysis.

Set 508 to win, England was 0-50 before losing both openers, Mike Atherton lbw and Stewart bowled, beginning a familiar procession whenever Warne was around.

Stewart had struck a loose Warne delivery for four earlier in the over and seeing another flatter one, assumed it was a long hop and went into a pull shot, only to realise too late that it was the deadly flipper, Warnie's quicker one. It zeroed in and hit his middle and off stumps with Stewart still halfway through his bat swing.

The look of anguish on his face reminded of Mike Gatting at Old Trafford 18 months earlier.

The enormity of Warne's spell over the Englishmen was such that Stewart and Atherton borrowed sets of binoculars and sat up high in the stand with the Channel 9 cameraman trying to find a clue to his variations.

Warne's first seven overs in the first innings cost seven and his first eight overs in the second innings cost nine, the Englishmen crease bound and conservative, tying themselves in knots.

The Aussies had just returned from Pakistan where Warne and Tim May were constantly challenged by batsmen leaving their crease and looking to punish the half-volleys.

"It was such a stark difference to the way the Pakistanis had played," said Australian paceman Damien Fleming, 12th man in the match.

Other cricket writers have their say about Warnie's most significant balls:

ROBERT CRADDOCK:

"The Gatting ball will live on forever, but almost as special was the flipper which castled Alec Stewart at the 'Gabba and Basit Ali bowled between his legs on the final ball one night at the SCG (1995-96). It was Warnie at his theatrical and match-swinging best."

JON PIERIK:

"Two of the most memorable I've seen were the wickets of Andrew Strauss (bowled) at the MCG and Kevin Pietersen (bowled) in the second dig in Adelaide, both in 2006-07. Strauss had just reached 50 and looked to be finally regaining his touch when he played all round a leggie. It was Warne's 700th wicket all up, including the Rest of the World Test. Pietersen had played brilliantly against the Australians in England and had made two big scores in the first three innings of the Tests only to be bowled by a big leggie playing a shot which probably won't make his greatest-hits video. It was a huge wicket which broke England's back on that dramatic fifth day."

Ten Moments
He'd Like To Have Back

From a bit of hi-jinx around a
swimming pool to a century squandered...

1 Mooning hotel guests from a window in Darwin during his Cricket Academy days (1990). It resulted in him being sent back, via coach to Adelaide, a bumpy, exhausting, two-day marathon. After further disciplinary indiscretions he was suspended altogether.

2 Abusing Andrew Hudson. *Picture left* (Johannesburg, 1993).

3 Befriending "John" the bookmaker in Colombo (1994).

4 Breaking his right thumb when struck by a rearing delivery from Curtly Ambrose at Queens Park in Trinidad (1995). His hand blew up to almost twice its size.

5 Being outvoted 2-1 by his fellow selectors at St John's and missing the opportunity to take part in the Frank Worrell Series decider at Antigua (1999). Instead of his usual upfront role, the only time he ventured onto the oval was to play some casual tennis in front of the rooms with another reserve, Matt Elliott, during the tea interval.

Left: Johannesburg, 1994: a brain snap

6 Grassing Damien Fleming's hat-trick catch (v India, Adelaide, 1999-2000). He took some blinders at first slip in his time and this one, from Anil Kumble, was a gimme, easy pace, eye level, just to his right. Somehow Warne fluffed it. He was inconsolable afterwards. "He's taken some great catches for me this summer," said Fleming at the time. "He's allowed to drop one every now and again.""Flem" is not as magnanimous now! Only one Australian has taken two Test hat-tricks, Hugh Trumble, more than 100 years ago.

7 Confiscating a kid's bag after he had been sprung smoking in a non-smoking venue, Wellington's Westpac Trust Stadium (2000). Police intervened and Warne apologised. The maximum fine for being caught smoking in the stadium was $NZ10,000.

8 Being dumped as Australia's vice-captain for reasons other than cricket (2000).

9 Missing the sponsor's sign and a $1 million jackpot when he dispatched NSW's Stuart MacGill for six in a domestic one-dayer. "I think you've got it," said Blues wicketkeeper Brad Haddin as his leg-side hit soared closer and closer to the sign, only to just miss (2000-01).

10 Self-destructing on 99 against New Zealand in Perth (2001). He sat in a plastic chair in the shower room with all his gear on and didn't move for 20 minutes. He 11 times made half-centuries, without once going all the way to the century he so cherished. Later it was revealed that the bowler Daniel Vettori had over-stepped and the delivery should have been called a "no-ball".

Right: Sabina Park, 1995: full-throated

A Bit Of A Larrikin

"For a young leg-spinner he just about had it all. Warne 1991 was not too different from Warne now (1998) – a bit of a larrikin and an outstanding talent."
MARK TAYLOR

"I was shocked by Warne's comments. It was really terrible. With the agreement of my fellow umpire I called the Australian captain Allan Border over to discuss the young leg-spinner's appalling lapse."
DAVID SHEPHERD on the Hudson send-off (1994)

"Maybe, as with Posh Spice or Kylie Minogue, Warne is more famous than he is loved."
CHRISTIAN RYAN

"It took this particular Test match (at the 'Gabba, 1994-95) to fully convince me that a fellow with a penchant for Playboy undies was a once-in-a-lifetime bowler."
The ABC's KERRY O'KEEFFE

"Cricket and family life have never been easy bedfellows."
Ex-England fast bowler DEREK PRINGLE

"Warne does (sledge) and it is beneath contempt and no more than all his wonderful achievements shouldn't go unrecorded."
Ex-editor of *Wisden*, JOHN WOODCOCK

"No slow bowler ever worked an umpire so well. No slow bowler in my time ever got more lbws,"
MIKE ATHERTON

"Warne is more fragile than he seems and has suffered from losses of confidence, especially in India where the pitches turn slowly and batsmen are raised on dahl and spin."
PETER ROEBUCK

"The one section of the community where's Warne's popularity is unanimous is amongst the kids ... kids are good judges."
IAN CHAPPELL

Surprises, Sledges & Social Secretaries

*W*hen the laidback Jeff Thomson first captained Australia (West Indies, 1978), legend goes that he said: "I'm bowling, the rest of ya spread out!"

With Steve Waugh resting a minor ankle problem after Australia's 4–1 victory in the 2000 series one-dayers in New Zealand, Shane Warne, captaining his country for the first time at first-class level, virtually reversed the batting order with the Aussies needing less than 200 to defeat Northern Districts in Hamilton.

He came in at No.4 himself and promoted Brett Lee to five, Colin "Funky" Miller to six and Glenn McGrath to seven. The tail thought it was great ... and yes, Australia won!

*W*hen Tim May first met Warnie at the Cricket Academy in Adelaide (1990-91), he reckoned him to be little more than "a fat little blowie" and wondered at his physical capacity to do the hard stuff when required. WRONG!!!

*O*n the eve of Warnie's fairytale Ashes debut at Old Trafford (1993), commentator and ex-Test opener David Lloyd said he would far prefer off-spinner Tim May in Australia's opening Test XI. He was sure that the greenish wicket wouldn't suit a leg-spinner like Warne. OOPS!

They may have all been Test teammates but when Victoria play New South Wales, it's open season. Warnie was giving it to Michael Slater one day, so much so that Mark Waugh intervened and suggested his mate was going a little over the top.

"Go and blow dry your hair mate," said a pumped-up Warnie.

It was Warnie's first match for the Vics at the Junction Oval (1990-91) and he was very nervous as he took guard and seemed to take an eternity surveying the field. The West Australian 'keeper Tim Zoehrer certainly thought so: "Any chance of facing up Biscuit?" he said.

*W*arnie's hatred of vegetables and fruit is genuine. Once Steve Waugh stuck a half-eaten mushroom on top of his spaghetti bolognaise and pointed it out on Warne's return. He immediately started fretting and sweating, hating the idea of having swallowed even half a mushroom by accident. Maybe that was why he couldn't find a place for Waugh in his top 25 cricketers of his time!

*I*n the old days Australians players used to bunk together on tour. Ian Healy always said he always felt like Warnie's social secretary, so many phone calls did the spin sultan receive. Fans used to ferret out the room he was in and come knocking on the door at all hours, just to say hello.

*N*o-one could "work" an umpire quite like Warnie. Rudi Koertzen once rejected a string of lbw appeals and Warnie, half-serious, quipped: "What, can't you pick me either Rudi?"

*T*he Australians were in the Pakistan province of Multan, Inzamam-el-Haq's home turf and Warnie, as usual, was having none of the local cuisine. He hadn't eaten for two days and sent a runner out to buy a packet of potato crisps, only to find out that they were stale! So his fast continued.

In Bermuda one day, one of the local stars was all at sea against Warne's combo of differently-paced side and straight spinners. Turning to wicketkeeper Ian Healy, he said: "This bloke is a lot easier to read on Spin Cam!"

When one of his heroes and good friends, St Kilda football legend Trevor Barker died from cancer in 1996, Warnie cut short a US holiday to attend his funeral. So many attended that the old Moorabbin Town Hall was chockers.

Whenever Daryll Cullinan walked to the crease, Allan Border would always say: "Warm up Shane," even if he didn't intend to bowl him immediately, so phobic was Cullinan about Warne's appearance at the crease.

Englishman Robin Smith was another to struggle against Warne, once conceding to wicketkeeper Ian Healy that he had "no idea which way they were going". A powerhouse right-hander, his career average was 43 but in his only series against Warne and the Aussies in '93, he averaged just 28 and was dropped.

One who tended to play him better than most was Pakistan's Salim Mailk, who in the '94 series, exposed all three stumps against Warne, taking guard wide of leg stump to help counter his curve and angle.

Salim, of course, was a little different. He also happened to be one of the ultimate dogs of cricket, who sold the game out ...

They Said It

"Warnie's idea of a balanced diet is a cheeseburger in each hand."
IAN HEALY

"We will never seen anything closer to perfection."
MIKE ATHERTON on Warne.

"Warnie is great to face because he gives you respect.
If you do well against him he is not one to give you abuse.
He will just say 'shot' and after a game or
a day's play he will come in and say 'well played'."
MICHAEL VAUGHAN

"He (Warnie) sent a Japanese restaurant into a panic one day when
he totally brushed the teriyaki and tempura to order a pizza!"
GLENN McGRATH

"The odds are it will be a boy with red hair and a toasted cheese
sandwich held in its right hand."
STEVE WAUGH on the impending birth of Warne's first child (1997).

"The mark of a champion is often the strength to overcome
disappointment. Warne took some stick in India but never lost heart,
or belief in himself."
JIM MAXWELL

"It is eight years now since the Gatting ball
but the effect remains. Warne has had an operation on his
spinning finger and another on his bowling shoulder and
he remains one of the most significant bowlers of the century."
RICHIE BENAUD (2001)

"One minute he's banging on about the slider and the flipper, the next
minute he's talking about 'cab sav-merlot blends'."
JOHN STERN (2003)

Betrayed

No bigger name in Australian cricket has ever been sacked like Warnie was in the Caribbean in 1999

Only once was Shane Warne ever dropped, amid a tumultuous few months in which he all but retired.

Shane Warne felt betrayed. Here he was in a cricketing paradise, the pivotal player in a world champion outfit and being told that he wasn't playing in the deciding Test.

He'd been outvoted by captain Steve Waugh and coach Geoff Marsh and he was ropable.

While others mingled with just-arrived Aussie supporters, enjoying news from home, Warne was stern-faced and surly. He couldn't mask his disappointment and soon retreated to the team's mini-bus.

Our tour group, from Kevin Dale's National Network Travel, had witnessed one of the great Tests in Barbados, when Warne, bowling in tandem with Stuart MacGill operated against Brian Lara with as many as seven players on the fence. Having fast-tracked his comeback after shoulder surgery to try and match the spectacular feats of leg-spinning replacement MacGill, for the first time in his career his form had deserted him.

Physically he was fine. But mentally, he was still in rehab. And the harder he tried the less effective his leg-break seemed to be. Even the normally-reviving influence of the spin doctor Terry Jenner hadn't

MENTOR: *Terry Jenner in the Caribbean in 1999*

worked. As Australia's vice-captain he'd had a vote too, and talked passionately about being able to lift when it counted. But the West Indies had stacked their top-order with left-handers and Waugh, 1-2 down, wanted a more balanced attack. The inclusion of another leftie in the West Indian squad, Wavell Hinds, tipped him over the edge. Warne was out and the offie Colin "Funky" Miller in. Never before or since had Waugh or Marsh had to make as tough a cricketing decision.

In the lead-up to Barbados, Warne had done all his practising in the centre in the actual matches, no practice facilities of worth being available anywhere in the Caribbean until the tour reached tiny Antigua. The day before the game, he bowled just 12 balls to wicketkeeper Ian Healy, after everyone else had gone in.

Most of us thought the best way to get back into form was to bowl for a couple of hours, like he used to do in the nets back at the Junction. But he spent more time having some throw-downs with coach Marsh and doing slip catching practice before watching on as a few of us had a trundle at Justin Langer and Michael Slater.

I actually slid a slow leggie past Langer and Warnie, watching on from deep gully, said in surprise, "wait a minute". But any joy was short-lived as Slater put one high, wide and handsome straight back over my head into the nearby fields. It went so far that it deserved to be a "12". I was bowling alongside Funky and he said: "Master, that might be it."

Come the Test the next day, to the third ball he faced from Neremiah Perry, Slater danced down the wicket and almost hit it straight over the George Challenor Grandstand. Marg Milne, one of our tour party turned to me and said: "Piessey, you must have played him into form!"

Warnie struggled to have any impact, the lefties Lara and Ridley Jacobs defeating him. He even missed a rendezvous with Jenner, who had come armed with the very bottle of Coonawarra St George wine Warne had presented him as a thank-you back in '92.

The decision made, I was at the team's luxury hotel in St John's, due to speak with Ian Healy who was contributing a foreword to one of my books. He'd been injured and dropped a catch that mattered in the final minutes at Barbados and was catching some zeds. Adam Gilchrist had flown in early to be on standby, but thought it was a long shot that he'd be called in. "He (Healy) is one of the toughest men in cricket," he said in the foyer. "He'll get up."

Warnie was spending the afternoon laying low. Never before in Australian cricket had such a big-name player been axed. Don Bradman was, but he was 20 at the time and had played only one Test. Much-loved Keith Miller was controversially omitted from the post-war tour of South Africa for bowling bouncers at the Don. But he ended up going anyway, his best years still to come. Warne was 29 and soon to be acknowledged as one of the five outstanding cricketers of the century by the cricketing bible *Wisden*. His near-record 317 wickets were a monument to his standing in the game.

His wife, Simone, said he didn't have anything more to prove. It would be nice to have him around home more often. It would certainly save on their phone bill.

And even after some encouraging efforts during the one-day

series in the Caribbean, Warne remained undecided. The controversies were wearing him down and with a young family, his priorities rapidly changing. No longer was cricket his all-consuming passion.

Weeks later, in London for the World Cup, he walked with Steve Waugh in a park, talking of the constant pressure and happenings which had made his life a soap opera. He wasn't bowling with his old confidence and was seriously thinking of quitting there and then. Waugh suggested he play through the tournament, go home and talk it over with his family. There was no need to make such a momentous decision so far from home.

Against the odds, the slow-to-start Australians had progressed through to the semi-finals and were playing South Africa at Edgbaston. It was June 15 and the rowdies in the Eric Hollies Stand were in fine voice early, predicting an Aussie exit and more punishment for Warne.

Somehow, the Australians, behind all day, forced a tie, Warne having told the players just before they walked out that if Australia lost, that was it. He was retiring.

"It was do or die time," Warne said in a Channel 9 interview.

"I had to know, under pressure, whether I could do it or not."

His 4-29 inspired one of the great comebacks in the most remembered one-day finish of all. Some of his leg breaks turned back the clock to 1993 and 1994. The Australians advanced and five days later, won the final against Pakistan in front of a sellout 30,000 crowd at Lord's. With another "four-for", Warne was again Man of the Match. The King was back, his reign just beginning ...

Big Names To Be Dropped

Shane Warne	1999	Bill Lawry	1970-71
Ricky Ponting	1996-97	Graham McKenzie	1967-68
Steve Waugh	1990-91	Don Bradman	1928-29
Doug Walters	1972		

Shane By Shane III

NAIVE "I was standing there with beer and pie in hand watching the (MCG Test) cricket when Australian team coach Bob Simpson and media manager Ian McDonald walked past. 'Set for the day Shane?' they asked. I had a lot to learn... The news was out that I'd been chosen to replace Peter Taylor in the next Test in Sydney." (1991)

PHILOSOPHY (1) "I'm a spinner with a fast bowler's mentality. I like to stir the batsmen. I have to tease them, try to deceive them. Torment them."

PHILOSOPHY (2) "Everybody is good at something."

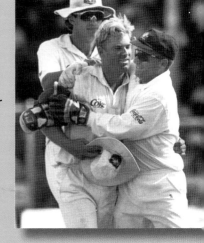

SELF-BELIEF "I know that when Shane Warne's at his best, he's the best leg-spinner in the world. My record proves that." (1999)

ON PRIVACY "At the end of the day the game has cost me a hell of a lot in my personal life."

SELF-CRITICAL "I have done a few stupid things along the way, on and off the field. There are some people who think I am a bit of an idiot and at times I would have to admit they've been right."

ON SLEDGING "Allan Border taught me the usefulness of sledging, in raising my own game. If things were not happening for me, he suggested that it was probably worth having a word with the batsman – not for the sake of having a go, but to switch myself on for the contest."

22 Things You Might Not Know About Warnie

From skulling spirits and pints to some by-play with umpire Aleem Dar in his final Test ...

1 At the age of eight Shane Warne broke both legs when a kid jumped on him at school. At one stage he was in plaster from the waist down and for almost 12 months, could only get around on a small trolley.

2 His first competitive cricket was played for the East Sandringham Boys. An East Sandy player, Ron Cantlon, first showed him how to grip a leg break.

3 He won a sports scholarship to Mentone Grammar in year 10.

4 His mates called him "Twistie" at school, for his strawberry blond locks. Less complimentary was "Showbags". Another early nickname was Hollywood, compliments of his St Kilda football mate Trevor Barker. "Barks" always felt Warnie was larger than life. He was also called "Truman" after the Jim Carrey lead character in *The Truman Show* (Carrey was filmed 24 hours a day) and *Elvis*, an Ian Healy nickname after all the hysteria for him in South Africa in 1994. Greg

Matthews dubbed him "Suicide" after the INXS hit, *Suicide Blonde*.

5 His heroes were all footballers, especially the flamboyant, strutting, cavorting Dermott Brereton, whose No.23 Warnie wore on the back of his favourite brown and gold Hawthorn jumper.

6 He played one open-age game with St Kilda at reserves level against Carlton, but was struggling with flu and ended up on the bench. He was never selected again. In one Under 19s match at Geelong, he was reported for striking and received a two-week sentence, suspended for a two-year period.

7 Playing for the first time overseas, with the Imperials and Knowle cricket clubs in Bristol in 1989, he stacked on more than 15 kg in five months. It was one helluva party.

8 He was one of the first leading high-profile sportsmen to first wear an earring, a Nike swooch after one of his early sponsors. He liked it that one of the few others was basketball superstar Michael Jordan.

9 He likes to drive fast cars. His Ferrari sounded like a mosquito as it zipped down Brunton Avenue directly outside the MCG after one afternoon practice session.

10 Almost 200 guests attended his marriage at historic Como House in South Yarra (1995). Security guards were hired to keep the media away.

11 In his only ever representative match on synthetic turf, at the Kowloon CC in Hong Kong in May, 1997, 20 balls go for 43 (he does take two wickets). Sunil Gavaskar's son, Rohan, makes an unbeaten 51 from only 30 balls

12 He was in England in '97 when his first child, Brooke was born and in Wales when his son Jackson was born. The Aussies celebrated the birth that night with an impromptu party at their Wales hotel by skulling spirits and pints.

13 He had to withdraw from a season with Hampshire in 2003 after his drugs ban, with NSW's Simon Katich among those to take his place. Season 2008 is his scheduled final year at Hants, when he is due to turn 39.

14 In a triumphant return to international cricket in 2004 he took 70 wickets in 12 Tests, Australia winning 10 of them.

15 A British tabloid once offered 25,000 pounds for him to pose in a jockstrap. Another paper offered him five figures to pose topless. Both lures were refused.

16 Mark Taylor was responsible for 51 of his 702 "pure" Test wickets, from first slip, the most taken by a fieldsman from the bowling of the boy from Black Rock.

17 His portrait, painted by English artist Fannie Rush hangs in the Long Room bar at Lord's.

18 When he took his 600th Test wicket, he kissed a wrist band given to him by eight year-old-Brooke, back in Melbourne with her mother. On the band was the word STRENGTH. Brooke had told her Dad that in their absence, he had to be strong.

19 A book of 28 Warnie tribute poems by a Melbourne bed-and-breakfast owner Victoria Coverdale was self-published in 2006. Here is a sample:

> *Mike Gatting's mouth became an 0*
> *With a single delivery which changed the world*
> *Mike's, Shane's and mine you know*

20 In his farewell Test in Sydney (2007), he told umpire Aleem Dar not to worry where his feet were landing on the popping crease. "Just take care of what is happening at the other end mate!"

21 No-one has appeared as often in winning teams: Sydney, 2007 was his 91st victory in pure Test cricket, 92 if you count Australia's "Test" v an ICC World XI in 2005.

22 Warnie made 34 ducks, a very high number for someone good enough to score 12 Test 50s and average 17-plus. Only Glenn McGrath (35) and the great West Indian No.11 Courtney Walsh (43) made more.

A Master Of Puppets

"Along the way Warne explained the prodigious powers of his slider, back-spinner and zooter. After landing the zooter veers neither left nor right. The slider has many of the same attributes ... Curiously the back spinner is likewise minded."
PETER ROEBUCK

"I overheard a conversation between Richie and Shane Warne one day on the spinning axis of the flipper ... when kids on the street are referring to 'sliders' and trying to produce them with tennis balls then we are winning."
Former England captain TONY LEWIS

"There was controversy during the series about utterances from Shane Warne who was heard on air to sledge ... The incident prompted some amusing letters. I see that Channel Nine cameraman is back, getting poor old Shane in trouble again."
The ABC's JIM MAXWELL

"Because he can spin the ball so much, he can pitch it so wide of leg stump you can't tread on it and often you cannot judge the turn well enough to put a pad in the way."
RAY ILLINGWORTH

"Warne says to me, 'Well played Mr Gooch'.
He addresses me as Mr Gooch, he says it's as 'a mark of respect of skill and age', but I think he overdoes it."
GRAHAM GOOCH

"It was ironic he should end the home series against South Africa by taking Richard Snell's wicket with a return catch off a full toss. It was one of the very few full tosses Warne bowled all summer."
PHILLIP DERRIMAN

Cricket's Human Headline

A 20-year timeline from St Kilda to Sydney

1987-88: Invited to St Kilda Cricket Club by his school sportsmaster and first XI opening batsman Andrew Lynch, Warnie debuts in the club's fourth XI as a batsman and occasional bowler. "You could never have told then where he would be now," says Lynch. "We always thought, though, if he could land them, he could be anything."

1988: Has a season of football with St Kilda Under 19s where he is tagged "Young Barks" for his bleached, blond hair. Plays one game in the reserves before being delisted.

1988-89: Makes four from No.4 and takes 2-46 in the third XI Grand Final against Richmond. Captain Geoff Tamblyn says: "He was fantastic to play with. You knew he was going to be good."

1989: Plays in the UK for the first time in Bristol; starts the Melbourne club season in the thirds before being promoted through to the first XI by round five. Plays in a roller-coasting Grand Final in which St Kilda is beaten by just three runs. Is in the crucial last partnership with captain Shaun "The Fuhrer" Graf, who goes out with just a boundary needed. Warnie still reminds Graf now that had he been allowed to play his shots, the Saints would have won by a wicket! Is invited with fellow Saint Laurie Harper to the Australian Institute of Sport's Cricket Academy in Adelaide.

1990-91: Is sent home, by bus, from Darwin back to Academy headquarters in Adelaide after a lark around a hotel swimming pool. Following further discipline breaches, he's suspended by the AIS's Robert de Castella and returns to Melbourne where almost immediately he's added to Victoria's senior training squad. Makes his first-class debut against Western Australia in Melbourne. Plays in St Kilda's 1990-91 senior VCA premiership team.

January, 1992: Selected for Australia after just a handful of first-class matches with Victoria, his first-up figures blow-out to an embarrassing one for 150 against India in Sydney. So under-prepared is he that he bowls virtually only his leg break variations. Is too scared to try his googly.

1993: With his hair dyed jet blond, Warne produces his famed "Ball of the Century" at Old Trafford which skittles a disbelieving Mike Gatting. It's his first delivery in an Ashes Test. "My goodness me," says Richie Benaud in the BBC commentary box.

March, 1994: Having been hit by an orange and copped a barreling from the partisan Wanderers crowd in Johannesburg, Warne explodes in an unsavoury send-off of South Africa's Andrew Hudson. Is fined his entire match fee of $4400 after the umpires had originally docked him just $400.

September, 1994: Down $US5000 on roulette at a Colombo casino, Warne accepts a large cash gift from an Indian cricket fan, called "John" and promptly loses that as well. It's the first step in a match-fixing furore which is to cost Warne, and fellow high-profiler Mark Waugh money, credibility and influence.

1994-95: Warne takes a first-ever hat-trick in front of an adoring Melbourne home crowd as England is dismissed for just 92 to go 2-0 down in a lopsided Ashes battle. With 20 wickets in the first two Tests, Warne is unstoppable.

February, 1995: Warne is fined $500 after contravening International Cricket Council regulations by wearing a black wristband with a sponsor's name on it during the third Australia v New Zealand international at Dunedin.

September 1995: Marries his sweetheart Simone Callahan from Ascot Vale at Como House in trendy South Yarra. He had proposed two years previously during Australia's tour of the UK.

1997-98: In his new role as treasurer and executive member of the Australian Cricketers' Association, Warne is party to the militant action and a set of potential strike dates laid down by the ACA after a breakdown in their salary and welfare negotiations with the Australian Cricket Board.

December, 1997: Warne walks out of a Melbourne function in which his extra weight is questioned and threatens to black-ban the media. He tells journalists the interest in his weight is over the top, petty and nothing at all to do with the good cricket he is producing.

January 1998: Jacques Kallis pads up to a Warne over-spinner and is bowled through the gate. It is the spin king's 300th wicket and one of 11 in a memorable start to the New Year against Hansie Cronje's South Africans in Sydney.

Winter, 1998: Has two operations to repair his over-worked shoulder. Specialists say that had he attempted to play even one or two more games at the tail-end of Australia's extended 1997-98 season that his shoulder could have become so damaged that he would never have been able to bowl again.

> *"The more I watch Shane Warne, the more I am convinced he will make a wonderful Australian captain."*
> ALLAN BORDER

1998-99: Having been named Victoria's new cricket captain, Warne immediately lands himself in trouble and is fined his entire match fee of $2400 after slamming the standard of umpiring, especially an lbw decision against Graeme Vimpani in an early-season Sheffield Shield game. Bowls himself sparingly coming back from his operations and is ruled out of early Ashes series battles. Plays only the last Test, enough to ensure his selection to the Caribbean.

The switchboard at Victoria's cricket headquarters is jammed with people calling for Warne's sacking as state captain after news of his association with "John" the bookmaker is uncovered. The headlines in the *Herald Sun* trumpets DAY OF SHAME. *The Australian*'s front page story is headlined CRICKET STARS HUMILIATE NATIONAL GAME. Experts query why news was withheld that Warne had been fined $8000 for accepting money from bookmakers.

April, 1999: On the eve of the Frank Worrell trophy series decider in St. Johns, Warne is dropped after under-performing in Barbados. Warne, Australia's vice-captain, votes for himself but coach Geoff Marsh and captain Steve Waugh trump him. "It was just about the toughest decision I've ever had to make," says Waugh. It's the first time since his earliest international days that he'd lost his place in Australia's best XI.

Warne is snapped by a *News of the World* photographer smoking when he was meant to be abstaining.

1999-2000: Still stewing at the disappointment of forfeiting the Victorian captaincy, Warne is accused of muttering: "Can't bowl, can't throw" in reference to the performance of Test newcomer Scott Muller from Queensland. While a Channel 9 cameraman takes the rap, Muller further fuels the controversy by continuing to accuse Warne.

March, 2000: Warne walks off Wellington's Westpac Trust Stadium (the old Basin Reserve) to a guard of honour having claimed his 356th Test wicket, topping previous Australian record-holder Dennis Lillee. "It was one of the most exhilarating moments of my life," he says.

Winter, 2000: Unhappy at the furore over Warne's very public phone sex affair with a nurse during his first year of English county cricket, the ACB strips Warne of the Australian XI vice-captaincy.

2002-03: Despite dislocating his shoulder in a one-dayer at the MCG, Warne defies initial opinion and returns just five weeks later. "He's a quick healer," says his brother and manager Jason.

January 2003: Is flown home on the eve of Australia's World Cup campaign after testing positive to a banned substance. Is suspended for 12 months for a violation of Cricket Australia's drug code. Later admits to several times taking his mother's slimming pills so he could look good on television. Withdraws an intended appeal when it is learnt that the re-opening of the case could see his time on the sidelines doubled. Several sponsors withdraw their support, unhappy to be linked with a so-called drug "cheat". Phil O'Meara and County cricket bats remain loyal, however, paying him his normal $50,000 a year, even though he wasn't playing anywhere.

Summer, 2003-04: Is told by his wife and mother of his three children, Simone, he is on his "last chance" after a Melbourne stripper goes public about an alleged affair; takes 72 wickets in a triumphant return to Test cricket; announces the formation of The Shane Warne Foundation to assist under-privileged kids.

March, 2004: Having served his suspension, Warne becomes the first Australian to take 500 Test wickets, during the first Test against Sri Lanka in Galle - the first of three remarkable comeback Tests in which he claims 26 wickets.

July, 2004: Warne equals Muthiah Muralidaran's Test wickets record in Cairns, taking 10 wickets in two winter Tests to lift his aggregate to 527. The ball with which he took his 527th wicket (Sri Lanka's Upul Chandana) is signed and inscribed and later auctioned on eBay.

2005: Streaks ahead of Murali, taking a record 96 wickets for the calendar year, including 40 in the climatic Ashes series in England; admits his marriage is "on the rocks" after more reports of sex on the side.

December, 2006: Announces his Test retirement on the eve of the Melbourne Test in which he takes his 700th wicket. Says he would have retired 18 months earlier but for Australia losing the Ashes; his divorce is formalised.

2007: Leads Hampshire again and is joined by Simone Callahan and their three young children for a large chunk of the English season; names India's Sachin Tendulkar as the No.1 player of his time in his column in *The Times* in London. His first Test captain Allan Border comes in at No.4 and Mark Taylor at No.9. Controversially Steve Waugh is excluded from his top 25. Signs a six figure contract with Foster's to join David Boon as a VB ambassador. Thousands of Warnie dolls are produced, a slight irony given Warne's partiality for drinks other than beer!

Shane Warne's list
of the greatest cricketers of his time
from *The Times*, London, 2007

1. Sachin Tendulkar
2. Brian Lara
3. Curtly Ambrose
4. Allan Border
5. Glenn McGrath
6. Wasim Akram
7. Muthiah Muralidaran
8. Ricky Ponting
9. Mark Taylor
10. Ian Healy
11. Courtney Walsh
12. Mark Waugh
13. Anil Kumble
14. Rahul Dravid
15. Graham Gooch
16. Andrew Flintoff
17. Matthew Hayden
18. Merv Hughes
19. Aravinda de Silva
20. Adam Gilchrist
21. David Boon
22. Martin Crowe
23. Stephen Fleming
24. Brett Lee
25. Darren Lehmann
26. Steve Waugh
27. Jacques Kallis/ Shaun Pollock
28. Saeed Anwar/ Mohammad Yousuf
29. Shoaib Akhtar/ Craig McDermott
30. Kevin Pietersen
31. Tim May
32. Robin Smith
33. Allan Donald
34. Bruce Reid
35. Michael Vaughan
36. Andy Flower
37. Stephen Harmison
38. Sanath Jayasuriya
39. Stuart MacGill
40. Kapil Dev
41. Justin Langer
42. Ravi Shastri
43. Michael Atherton
44. Alec Stewart
45. Waqar Younis
46. Dilip Vengsarkar
47. Chris Cairns
48. Brian McMillan
49. Darren Berry
50. Jamie Siddons

HEROES ALL: the 2006-07
Ashes-winniung Aussies
Photo: Patrick Eagar

The Hidden Stats

WARNIE'S AUSTRALIAN RECORD

	Mts	Wkts	Ave	Best	5wl	10w	Strike-rt	Econ rt
Tests*	144	702	25.47	8-71	37	10	57	2.65
ODIs	194	293	25.75	5-33	1	-	36	4.25

* Pure Test matches included only

WARNIE IN TEST CRICKET

Opponent	Mts	Wkts	Ave	Best	5wl	10w	Strike-rt	Econ rt
Bangladesh	2	11	27.27	5-113	1	-	47	3.4
England	36	195	23.25	8-71	11	4	55	2.4
India	14	43	47.18	6-125	1	-	91	3.1
New Zealand	20	103	24.37	6-31	3	-	56	2.6
Pakistan	15	90	20.17	7-23	6	2	45	2.6
South Africa	24	130	24.16	7-56	7	2	60	2.3
Sri Lanka	13	59	25.54	5-43	5	2	53	2.8
West Indies	19	65	29.95	7-52	3	-	62	2.4
Zimbabwe	1	6	22.83	3-68	-	-	53	2.5

WARNIE ON AUSTRALIAN GROUNDS

Opponent	Mts	Wkts	Ave	Best	5wl	10w	Strike-rt	Econ-rt
Adelaide Oval	13	56	30.44	6-80	2	-	72	2.5
Brisbane	11	68	20.30	8-71	3	2	48	2.4
Cairns	1	7	28.42	4-70	-	-	64	2.6
Darwin	1	3	27.00	3-20	-	-	51	3.2
Hobart	6	28	22.17	6-31	3	-	49	2.1
Melbourne	11	56	23.34	7-52	3	-	56	2.4
Perth	12	37	36.45	4-83	-	-	77	2.8
Sydney	13	58	29.81	7-56	4	2	66	2.6

Stats to make your leggies curl, from the quirky and offbeat to the real McCoys

Not even Don Bradman was subject to the same fast-tracking as Shane Warne. First picked for Australia on potential rather than performance, 22-year-old Warne had taken only 26 first-class wickets, just 15 of them in Australia.

In the last 100 years, only one bowler has won Test selection at home with fewer first-class wickets in Australia: Newcastle leggie Johnny "Wok" Watkins (10 first-class wickets prior to Test debut in 1973) whose elevation ranks with the greatest mis-selections of all. Having bowled some of the widest wides ever seen in international cricket in his one and only Test at the Sydney Cricket Ground, Wok never played first-class cricket in Australia again.

The story of Warne's early struggles to survive included him not wanting to bowl his googly on debut in case it bounced twice. His bowling average peaked, briefly, at 346, the worst average ever suffered by any Australian bowler, ahead of Ian Chappell, whose average at one stage ballooned to 267.

Despite his riveting Test-turning spell of 3-0 in Colombo, it wasn't a career re-shaping performance. In essence, he had no particular plans or strategies back then. He just walked in and tried to spin you-know-what out of the ball.

He took no wickets in his next Test and became a fringe selection; he finished his first Test summer out of Victoria's best XI and there was even a Saturday spent with St Kilda seconds in those early international years.

His average still exceeded 100 before his breakthrough 7-52 at the MCG against the West Indies in 1992-93. Earlier that day he told teammate Ian Healy that he was worried he'd be hit all around the park in front of his mates and never be picked again!

From the time he flippered Richie Richardson, he became a phenomenon, taking 203 wickets at 22 in his next 40 Tests, until a finger operation interrupted his career in 1996.

Though still a potential match-winner, Warne was not quite the same bowler when he returned. In 40 Tests from late 1996 to 2000, interrupted again by a shoulder operation in 1998, he took 159 wickets at an average of 29.

Eventually, Warne learned to make up for the technical limits imposed by injury through smarter and more mature bowling. After recovering from a broken finger and a knee operation in 2000, he then took 125 wickets at 25 in his next 23 Tests, before being sidelined him again, this time over a bottle of slimming pills.

Returning from suspension in 2004, he reinforced his place among the great bowlers with 211 wickets in 37 Tests at 25. However, his last year, 2006, showed indications of fading powers, with his average exceeding 30.

WARNIE'S MILESTONE WICKETS*

1	Ravi Shastri (India), 1991-92, Sydney, his 1st Test
50	Nasser Hussain (Eng.), 1993, Trent Bridge, 14th
100	Brian McMillan (S. Afr.), 1993-94, Adelaide, 23rd
150	Steve Rhodes (Eng), 1994-95, Melbourne, 31st
200	Chaminda Vass (Sri Lanka), 1995-96, Perth, 42nd
250	Alec Stewart (Eng.), 1997, Old Trafford, 55th
300	Jacques Kallis (S. Afr.), 1997-98, Sydney, 63rd
350	Hrishikesh Kanitkar (India), 1999-00, Melbourne, 80th
356	Paul Wiseman (NZ), 1999-2000, Auckland, 82nd
	(breaking Dennis Lillee's all-time Test wickets record)
400	Alec Stewart (Eng.), 2001, The Oval, 92nd
450	Ashwell Prince (S. Afr.), 2001-02, Durban, 101st
500	Hashan Tillakaratne (Sri Lanka), 2003-04, Galle, 108th
550	James Franklin (NZ), 2004-05, Adelaide, 117th
600	Marcus Trescothick (Eng.), 2005, Manchester, 126th
650	Mark Boucher (S. Afr.), 2005-06, Melbourne, 133rd
700	Steve Harmison (Eng.), 2006-07, Melbourne, 143rd
702	Andrew Flintoff (Eng.), 2006-07, Sydney, 144th

"... Australia never once lost an Ashes Test when both Warne and McGrath played."

* Not including World XI matches. It is a pity that Warne's 700th wicket in "real" Tests, taken on the last day of his last Test on his home ground, in front of 80,000 people, went largely unnoticed.

AND SOME QUIRKY ONES TO FINISH

- Warnie won 17 Man of the Match awards in Tests, an Australian record, ahead of Steve Waugh and Ricky Ponting on 14, but one short of Muthiah Muralidaran's leading mark of 18.

- He is also the leading Australian with eight Player of the series awards, ahead of Steve Waugh with six. Murali leads everyone with 11.

- Warne has been hit for six at least 158 times in his Test career (there are possibly a handful of others not identified), more than any other bowler in history, and more than three times more than any other Australian. (Stuart MacGill is next with 46). The most successful six-hitters against Warne have been adopted Englishman Kevin Pietersen, with 10 and Kiwis Craig McMillan and Chris Cairns, seven apiece. Pietersen has also scored 307 runs from Warne's bowling, the most for any batsman from 1999 to 2007. He averaged 61.4 from his bowling.

- Perhaps his most extraordinary bowling sequence was 5-5 from 22 balls against South Africa at the SCG in 1993-94. It wasn't a case of "running through the tail" either. His victims included frontline trio Jonty Rhodes, Gary Kirsten and Kepler Wessels!

- The most runs off a Warne over came late in his career: 21 including two leg byes (0,6,6,2lb,6,1) by Mohammad Rafique of Bangladesh at Chittagong in 2005-06. Prior to that, in 1998, India's Mohammad Azharuddin took 18 from an over at Chennai. The sequence was: 4,0,4,4,0,6.

- An oddity of Warne's career is that success on his home ground was surprisingly limited. In senior cricket of all kinds, barely 10 per cent of Warne's 1700+ wickets have been taken on the Melbourne Cricket Ground. Warne has never taken 10 wickets in a first-class match on the MCG, and his name will not be found on a list of the 100 best (first-class) bowling performances at the ground. Warne's record in Tests at the MCG is weaker than in Sydney, Brisbane or Adelaide, or in Bangladesh, England, New Zealand, Pakistan, Sri Lanka, Zimbabwe and South Africa.

- Fashions change, even in cricket statistics. In 2005, when Shane Warne passed his hero Dennis Lillee's peak of 85 Test wickets in a calendar year, going on to a record 90 wickets (plus six in the World XI match), it was a major feature of newspaper and website reports. But when Lillee set his mark in 1981, nobody noticed and the record went unremarked in the major publications of the day. Warne actually took 96 wickets (102 including the World XI) in 273 days from July 21, 2005 to April 20, 2006, his most prolific sequence over any period of less than 365 days. Only Muralidaran has done better, with 113 wickets in the 365 days to July 23, 2002.

- Brian Lara once went for more than eight years (1997 to 2005) without being dismissed by Warnie in a Test. Lara was also undismissed by Murali from 1997 to 2001 and remains the No.1 batsman Murali has ever opposed.

- Warne's No.1 is India's Sachin Tendulkar, whom he regards as a God. He only ever dismissed him three times in 12 Tests, twice since 1999 when Tendulkar scored 170 runs against him, at an average of 85. In the same eight-year period, 1999-2007, Lara scored 222 runs from his bowling at an average of 74.

- Not one of the 120 batsmen dismissed by Warne from November, 2002 to October, 2004 scored a century.

- The average score of all batsmen dismissed by Warne is 23.6.

- Like most spinners, Warne took lower-order wickets by the 10s and 100s. Some 37.1 per cent of his wickets came against numbers 8-11 in the batting order. Among bowlers with more than 150 wickets, only India's Harbhajan Singh (38.7 per cent) and Stuart MacGill (38.9 per cent) have higher strike-rates against the tail. One reason modern Australian bowlers have high percentages is that Aussie teams have tended to bowl their opposition out, and therefore bowl to tail-enders, more often than most. Spin bowlers also tend to be opposed less against top-order batsmen, especially when those batsmen are failing.

- Warne's longest Test bowling spell was 41 overs, back in his youth, at Old Trafford in 1993. He bowled 37 over spells against Pakistan at Bellerive in 1999 and against South Africa at Cape Town in 2002, part of his 70 overs in that innings.

- Warne dismissed 236 different batsmen during his Test career, including Alec Stewart 14 times, Ashwell Prince and Nasser Hussain 11 and Mike Atherton 10.

- About 23.2 per cent of Warne's dismissals were left-handers. This is very similar to the proportion of left-handed batsmen overall, in Tests against Australia since 1991 (22.7 per cent).

- Warne's 40 wickets in the 2005 Ashes series was the most by any bowler for a losing side in a five-Test series.

- During his career, Warne was on the winning side 91 times (plus the World XI match), or 63 per cent of his Tests, with 26 losses. When Warne took five-wicket hauls, the Australians won 75 per cent of their Tests, but when Warne was absent, Australia's winning percentage dropped to 56 per cent. The effect of Warne's absence was greatly magnified if Glenn McGrath was also absent from the team. Australia never once lost an Ashes Test when both Warne and McGrath played. In their last 41 Tests together, Warne and McGrath lost only once, to South Africa in 2002, at Durban. Their last loss together in a home Test was in 1996-97 against West Indies at Perth.

- Over the last 10 years, Australia's bowling average when both Warne and McGrath were playing was 25.9. When both were absent, the team bowling average rose to 42.7 (ignoring Tests v Zimbabwe).

- Warne's last ball in Test cricket was hit to the boundary by Steve Harmison. His first, also in Sydney had been blocked by India's Sanjay Manjrekar. As he walked out that day as Australia's 350th Test cricketer, skipper Allan Border quipped to him: "Don't do a Johnny Watkins on us!" (a reference to Watkins' nightmarish beginning 20 years previously).

Warnie's Batting Order Test dismissals	
Position in order	
1-2	103
3	58
4	61
5	81
6	73
7	65
8	71
9	75
10	72
11	43
Total	702

- Warne's last Test may have been unremarkable with the ball, but in his 145th (or 144th) match, he did manage a personal batting first: it was the first time that he had made the highest individual innings (71) for Australia in a completed Test. He had previously top-scored for Australia in a drawn Test, when he scored 99 against New Zealand in Perth in 2002.

- Warne preferred batting in Australia: eight of his 12 half-centuries were scored at home, and his average was 19.2 at home versus 15.9 away.

- Warne is the only player to score more than 3000 Test runs without a century. Less well-known is another Warne batting "distinction": he faced, on average, 29.4 balls per dismissal in Tests, the shortest average innings length for any player with more than 2000 Test runs in history! Next on the list is Kapil Dev, 38 balls per dismissal.

- A puzzle from Warne's career: his performances were often mediocre when he was teamed with fellow leggie Stuart MacGill. In their 15 Tests together, Warne took 74 wickets at 29.6, while MacGill's return was 86 wickets at 22.1. MacGill outperformed Warne in 10 of those 15 games (plus in the World XI match, too). Warne's returns were inferior to his career as a whole, even though they were selected as a pair only when conditions supposedly favoured spin. By contrast, MacGill's bowling average when not paired with Warne ballooned from 22 to over 30.

- Although Warne went wicketless eight times in Tests, the last occasion was in early 2000, and he took at least one wicket in each of his last 63 Tests.

- A study of catches in Tests from 2001 to 2005 found reference to 15 dropped catches by Shane Warne; almost all at slip. But he took 46 catches over the same period. His drop rate of around 25 per cent was typical for Test cricket, although a little higher than Australia's average of 21 per cent. As a bowler, about 21 per cent of the chances off his bowling were dropped.

WARNIE'S RECORD HOME & AWAY

Opponent	Mts	Home wkts	Ave	Wkts per mt	Mts	Away wkts	Ave	Wkts per mt
England	14	66	25.81	4.71	22	129	21.94	5.86
South Africa	12	69	25.04	5.75	12	61	24.31	5.08
West Indies	12	48	26.52	4.00	7	17	39.64	2.42
New Zealand	11	54	27.16	4.90	9	49	21.30	5.44
India	5	9	62.55	1.80	9	34	43.11	3.77
Pakistan	9	45	21.55	5.00	6	45	18.80	7.50
Sri Lanka	5	22	32.40	4.40	8	37	21.45	4.62
Zimbabwe					1	6	22.83	6.00
Bangladesh					2	11	27.27	5.50
TOTAL	68	313	26.40	4.60	76	389	24.61	5.11

WARNIE'S TEST TEAMMATES

	Mts played
Shane "Hollywood" Warne	**144**
Glenn "Pidgeon" McGrath	103
Mark "June" Waugh	103
Steve "Tugga" Waugh	96
Ricky "Punter" Ponting	84
Justin "Alfie" Langer	76
Ian "Heals" Healy	74
Adam "Gilly" Gilchrist	69
Matthew "Haydos" Hayden	68
Mark "Tubby" Taylor	66
Michael "Slatts" Slater	60
Damien "Marto" Martyn	56
Jason "Dizzy" Gillespie	53
Greg "Blewie" Blewett	45
Brett "Bing" Lee	44
David "Boonie" Boon	44
Michael "Kasper" Kasprowicz	36
Craig "Billy" McDermott	35
Paul "Pistol" Reiffel	33
Allan "A.B." Border	26
Michel "Pup" Clarke	25
Matthew "Herb" Elliott	21
Michael "Bevo" Bevan	17
Merv "Swervin" Hughes	17
Simon "Cat" Katich	16
Darren "Boof" Lehmann	17
Tim "Maysie" May	17
Mike "Huss" Hussey	16
Stuart "Mac" MacGill	15
Damien "Flemo" Fleming	14
Andrew "Roy" Symonds	13

	Mts played
Stuart Clark	9
Colin "Funky" Miller	9
Andy "Bick" Bichel	8

Warnie also calls him "Bobby", as in Bob the Builder

	Mts played
Brendon "B.J." Julian	7
Brad "Bunk" Hodge	5
Jo "Joey" Angel	4
Dean "Ledge" Jones	4
Greg "Mo" Matthews	3
Gavin "Rid" Robertson	3
Mike "Roy" Whitney	3
Nathan "Andrew G." Bracken	2

(after the Aussie Idol host)

	Mts played
Simon "Snake" Cook	2
Phil "Pro" Jaques	2
Geoff "Swampy" Marsh	2
Tom "Long Tom" Moody	2
Scott Muller	2
Shaun "Bomb" Tait	2
Shane "Watto" Watson	2
Daniel Cullen	1
Adam "Chip" Dale	1
Tony "Dodders" Dodemaide	1
Phil Emery	1
Stuart Law	1
Peter "Macca" McIntyre	1
Bruce "Chook" Reid	1
Brad "Willo" Williams	1
Paul "Blocker" Wilson	1
Shaun "China" Young	1

*W*arnie may have joined the ranks of the retired, but he's everywhere, on mantels, TV sets and in your bedroom!

A new Warnie VB Doll, produced by the thousands, continues to be a Foster's marketing winner which has seen more than 400,000 Boony and Beefy dolls circulate as part of the VB "Boonanza".

The Warnie doll is similarly irreverent and interactive and has arrived just in time for summer. And there are a few cheeky lines, too, about mobile phones, adding to its sexiness and all-ages appeal.

VB consumers are interacting every day with the Warnie figurine. It becomes particularly animated during the one-day VB Series when the weather is at its warmest and cricket fans are at their thirstiest.

The Boony dolls included a 60-second sound chip containing more than 35 unique phrases and code words, ensuring Boony becoming a household name all over again. "Anyone seen my thongs?" Boony would ask. When he was feeling really energetic, he'd say: "I feel like playing totem tennis." It sold out within weeks.

Melbourne, 2007: With fellow VB ambassador David Boon.

eBay buyers have been parting with as much $220 for one of the original Boony dolls and "the Sultan of Spin" is proving just as appealing!

FURTHER READING

BOOKS

Darren Berry: *Keeping It Real, the Darren 'Chuck' Berry Story*, with Martin Blake (Bas Publishing, 2004)

Dickie Bird: *My Autobiography* (Hodder & Stoughton, 1997)

David Boon: *Boony's Ashes*, David Boon and Ken Davis (Wilkinson Books, 2006)

Ian Botham: *My Autobiography* (CollinsWillow, 1994)

Ian Chappell: *A Golden Age* (Pan Macmillan Australia, 2006)

Jack Egan,: *One who will, the search for Steve Waugh* (Allen & Unwin, 2004)

Andrew Flintoff: *Being Freddie, my story so far* (Hodder and Stoughton, 2005)

Graham Gooch: *My Autobiography* (CollinsWillow, 1995)

Darren Gough: *Dazzler, the autobiography* (Michael Joseph, 2001)

Ian Healy: *Hands and Heals*, with Robert Craddock (Harper Sports, 2000)

Ian Healy: *The Ian Healy Story*, Playing for Keeps (Swan Publishing, 1996)

Nasser Hussain: *Playing with fire, the autobiography* (Michael Joseph, 2004)

Ray Illingworth: *One Man Committee* (Headline Book Publishing, 1996)

Tony Lewis: *Taking Fresh Guard* (Headline Book Publishing, 2003)

Dennis Lillee: *Lillee: An Autobiography* (Headline Book Publishing, 2003)

Jim Maxwell: *Stumps* (Hardie Grant and Media 21 Publishing, 2001)

Glenn McGrath: *Pacemaker, the inner thoughts of Glenn McGrath*, with Daniel Lane (Pan McMillan, 1998)

Ken Piesse: Warne, *Sultan of Spin* (Modern Publishing, 1995)

Ken Piesse: *The Complete Shane Warne* (Viking, 2000)

Ken Piesse: *Cricket's Greatest Scandals* (Viking, 2000)

Paul Reiffel: *Reiffel Inside Out*, with Greg Baum (HarperSports, 1998)

Remembering Hookesy (Swan Sport, 2004)

Jonathon Rice: *The Fight For the Ashes* (Methuen Publishing, 2001)

Peter Roebuck: *Sometimes I Forgot to Laugh* (Allen & Unwin, 2004)

David Shepherd: *Shep, My Autobiography*, with David Foot (Orion Books, 2001)

Mark Taylor: *Time to Declare*, with Ian Heads (Pan McMillan, 1999)

Michael Vaughan: *A Year in the Sun* (Hodder and Stoughton, 2003)

Shane Warne: *My Own Story*, with Mark Ray (Swan Publishing, 1997)

Shane Warne: My Autobiography, with Richard Hobson (Hodder & Stoughton, 2001)

Mark Waugh: *A Year To Remember*, with Grantlee Keiza (Random House, 1997)

Steve Waugh: *Ashes Diary 1997* (HarperCollins, 1997)

ANNUALS

The ABC Australian Cricket Almanac, edited by Phillip Derriman (1994 edition)

Wisden Cricketers' Almanack

The Australian Wisden

MAGAZINES & SOUVENIR BROCHURES

Cricketer magazine

English Cricket Board souvenir programs 2001 & 2005

New Idea

The ABC Cricket Book

The Bulletin

The Cricketer International

The Wisden Cricketer

ABOUT THE AUTHOR, KEN PIESSE

*A*uthor, commentator and occasional leg-spinner Ken Piesse has been a Warne watcher ever since 16-year-old Shane had him stumped in a school match at Keysborough.

He was sitting in the old cigar stand at the 'G when Warnie flippered out Richie Richardson. He was there when Warnie took his one and only hat-trick courtesy of the "Keg on Legs" David Boon and he was there in the Caribbean when Warnie was dumped from Australia's Test team.

He has written two previous books about Warne and Warnie has contributed two forewords to his. He first hired him, too, as a celebrity writer for his *Cricketer* magazine.

Unlike Warnie whose leg-breaks spun viciously, Ken's were more friendly and resulted in him playing 10 consecutive years with Frankston Peninsula's third XI, without even once being promoted.

Among his most recent cricket books are *Cricket's Colosseum, 125 Years of Test Cricket at the MCG* and *The Ashes, an Illustrated History of the Game's Greatest Rivalry.*

Melbourne, 1987: The author at the 'G, flanked by Prime Minister Bob Hawke.

Index

TABLES

ON YA WARNIE